BALANCED WAY OF *life*

V V RAMPAL

INDIA • SINGAPORE • MALAYSIA

ISBN 979-8-89233-909-4

Also by the Same Author

1. A Bunch of Thoughts
2. A Stream of Thoughts
3. Musings of a Free Mind
4. Short Stories for the Young and Growing
5. Beliefs of a Reasoning Mind
6. A Dialogue on God
7. Belief, Reality and Spiritual Practice

Acknowledgement

I heartily thank Dr G P Kaushal for providing intellectual and technical support, for reading the manuscript and offering useful suggestions. I also thank Dr Nivita for providing technical support without which I would have faced many difficulties.

Summary

We nourish our body and mind with food and learning. In the modern world of stressful life we need to supplement this nourishment with the spiritual component as well. It will not only balance our individual life but will also improve the ethical environment that is fast eroding to extinction. The tensions generated by unspiritual activities need to be relieved by reintroducing the spiritual element into our daily living. We need to spare a moment for the invisible 'Supreme Power' that is behind every being. The book gives a glimpse of this aspect and addresses the way we can balance our life by including ethics and spirituality as necessary part of our life.

About the Author

Dr Rampal has worked as a scientist for over thirty years and has deep interest in the spiritual side of life. For over two and half decades he has been writing on both science as well as the need to spiritualize, and balance out the negative tendencies that affect our life adversely. He has written several books emphasizing this aspect. He believes in humanism and right living. He is an ardent supporter of spirituality as a necessary part of our way of life.

Contents

1
Right Living

What is a balanced life? In my view, it is a life in which the physical, mental and spiritual equally contribute to our daily activities. Ours is a geophysical structure that acts and reacts to sense inputs. In the language of cybernetics, this structure is a biological machine. In this, each physical part has a mechanical counterpart. The mind works like the software of the brain. Only the spiritual has no visible equivalent. This is because western scientific thought does not recognize the religious view of soul or spirit. However, over centuries and millennia, the spiritual aspect of life has caught the imagination and belief of people around the world. Much against opinions otherwise, belief in soul or spirituality persists in many parts of the world. It is supported by the religious philosophies of many faiths. One may believe or not, spirituality definitely plays an important role in our life and it is an important aspect of our working personality.

Most of us neglect spiritual aspect in our life because we are either too busy or too stressed to think about it. We are preoccupied with the need to maintain our body and mind and give no thought to the need of nourishing our soul as much as we nourish our body and mind. Our first priority is to keep our body in good health by feeding it sufficiently. This is particularly more important for those whose work requires muscle power.

We spend a good amount of time in information gathering to make us fit for earning our bread and seeking a respectful status. To fulfill the requirements of body and mind, we spend our whole life running from pillar to post, vigorously trying to make us a successful person. However, success is a relative term. It depends on what measure we adopt to define it. I may be called a successful person if I earn good grades in school and college, including the professional one, and get a good job and have a loving family that satisfies my emotional needs. But is it all that I seek in life? Are there not any higher aims or ambitions? Are we satisfied with this definition of success in life? Spirituality gives us a higher purpose in life.

Even if we achieve what we believe as success in life, what about the problems that are generally inevitable and make us sad and unsatisfied with our performance? We often blame our destiny or fate for our failures and remain at loss to understand the real cause of our imperfect life. Certainly there is something that we lack in our working that makes life incomplete and unbalanced.

We suffer occasional maladies in the family, emotional setbacks, shortage of resources to meet unexpected requirements, relatives' problems, accidental happenings and so on. It is under these situations that our preparations for life are tested. Most often we find ourselves ill-equipped to deal with them. We seek mental and physical support from others but in most cases that is not available since others too are sailing in the same boat. We seek help from visible or invisible sources but fail to appreciate that the real and permanent support lies within us. This support we often neglect due to our ignorance of our Self. This is what I refer to as the spiritual aspect of our being.

Now the question arises; what is spiritual in content, how to develop this content, how to make it a part of our life and how does it help us to sail smoothly over the obstructions and high winds in the sea of life? Is it possible to integrate this aspect in our day to day working life? Is it possible to merge it completely in our way of life without disturbing our mind body requirements?

Practically every religion has talked about a supreme all-powerful force that lies behind every activity in the universe. This force is an integral part of our existence. From an atom to the largest galaxy, from a nebula to the black hole, this mysterious force makes its presence felt in a way that is largely unexplained to complete satisfaction. A whole lot of literature is available on this mystery and every religion has evolved practices to seek help of this force for bettering our life. At the same time, there are persons of all hues who deny the existence of such a force and put this belief in the category of myth and ignorance. It is not my intention to get into this debate since intellect alone is not likely to decide the issue and reach the truth. In fact, intellect alone is not the guarantee of right living. Intellect must be alloyed with wisdom to be useful to society.

Ethical living is a part of spiritual way of life. All religious scriptures support this view. But modern intellectuals may deny this and say that ethics is essentially an outcome of intellectual thought. But one must understand that if it were so, the intellectual scientists would not invent mass-killing weapons. They have already done that and put the humanity in great danger. Moreover, they still keep doing so. Nowhere in the world has ethics involved killing of innocent people. The world has seen atomic holocaust and is still living under the fear of mass scale destruction. If our scientists, who certainly belong to the intellectual class, were the guardians of ethical way of life, they would not develop more and more destructive weapons and put our existence into jeopardy.

The essential ingredient of ethical living is to consider whole humanity as one family. Equality of all humans is the basis of it. We cannot treat people differently based on our convenience and personal gain. The idea of equality is divine in nature because nature provides its products equally to all without any distinction or favor. There is no denying the fact that everyone needs food, clothing and shelter and if anyone thinks otherwise, he or she is going against nature. Adhering to the principle of equality is the basic element of spirituality. Selfishness goes against the very root of ethical living. Anyone who lives for himself alone is actually violating the norms of right living.

Right living would therefore, involve not only our efforts to support the needs of body and mind but also the essential features of ethics and spirituality in the interest of all humanity. It ultimately affects the universal environment as well and makes our existence healthy, safe and fearless.

Right living in effect means providing food for mind, body and soul. We need good and wholesome food for body, and intellectual learning for the mind. Similarly, we need meditation and constant remembrance of the supreme power, or the ultimate reality, for the spiritual growth. This provides complete nourishment for right living in order to have right growth of human personality. In particular, spiritual growth needs faith in the Self; faith in the supreme power that is immanent in all beings. It is not necessary to be superstitious in order to be religious. One can be spiritual even though one does not believe in religious rituals and mythological beliefs. Faith however, acts an anchor in the troubled sea of practical life.

For right living, one spiritual person has given a simple formula that says 'Be good and do good'. It takes care, to a great extent, the ethical and spiritual side of your life without bothering you with long spiritual discourses that give you a long list of dos and don'ts.

To sum up what I have said so far, I restate as follows the essential three components of our personality which govern our behavior towards outside stimuli

O **BODY** it is the gross part made of flesh and bones that works like a machine. It requires food as input and provides muscle power to do physical activities. The physical activity can be good or bad depending on the intention of the doer.

O **MIND** it is the subtle part including intellect that uses ideas, memory, learning and imagination that enables intellectual pursuits. The mental activity also can be good or bad depending on the results it produces. It is a faculty that is too complex to define in simple terms since it is still a subject of scientific research.

O **SPIRITUAL** It is related to the spirit or soul and is the subtlest part of our being. It is also described in connection with inner light or pure consciousness, something that is known to be present in all human beings as the divine power. Its presence has been known, and experienced, by the spiritually elevated persons. Ethics and morality form an integral part of the spiritual element. A spiritual person is supposed to be selfless in action, act always for the good of others and shows the right path to people for a living that is free of tensions and troubles of the worldly life. Faith in the supreme power, prayer, worship, meditation and be good to all are the inputs required for the growth of this faculty.

2
FAITH

By faith here I mean trust in the words and deeds of an enlightened person. I do not use it in the sense of religion. Many people do not believe in religion for various reasons. Some do not like the beliefs and dictates; others do not believe in any supreme power other than the evolutionary nature of creation. Some hate the quarrels and violence that arise due to differences in religions. History of the world is filled with many battles and wars that arose on account of religious differences. This has certainly given a bad name to religion as such. But faith or trust is very important in our lives. Without faith in the cook, we would not eat what he or she cooks for us. Without faith in the teacher, or in the written word, we would not learn anything. Without faith in our spiritual masters, our progress in spirituality would not be possible. Even in politics or business, faith plays a great part. There will no mass following nor will any business deals materialize. Undoubtedly, faith therefore is an important part of our life.

Spirituality, in the first place, needs faith in the 'supreme Power'. This power is infinite, eternal, all-knowing and immanent in all beings. In common language it is known to be omnipotent, omniscient and omnipresent. This belief is the basis of building up the spiritual activity. Meditation is the instrument to strengthen this belief and raise the spiritual level to that of divinity.

This also coordinates the three aspects of our personality and brings a balance between the working of body and mind. Just as we like a clean surface to sit on, similarly we need to clean up our mind before meditation. We need to remove all extraneous thoughts and concentrate on one object or thought. That could be any of the many ways prescribed in the practice of spirituality. The whole idea is to raise the level of our consciousness to that of divine consciousness.

The experiences of the sages who meditated for long years have been recorded in the scriptures and form a philosophy of life. Vedanta is one such philosophy. It confirms the faith in the supreme power that is variously described in different religions. Vedanta calls it pure consciousness. It is commonly agreed that this supreme entity is the ultimate reality of all existence. Vedanta truths are not religion specific. In fact, they relate to all humanity. They treat the whole world as one big family and provide the basis for ethical and spiritual living.

Most religions have scriptural truths that emphasize a value-based living and that constitutes the spiritual content of that religion. It is only the rituals and mythology that differentiate one religion from another. Meditation on the supreme reality is common to most religions. Ethical norms originate from such sources and hence I call them divine in nature.

Some people give a human like form to the ultimate reality. It is only a convenience for meditation since it is much easier to concentrate on such a form than otherwise. Here again, faith comes in the picture. But for the enlightened ones, the reality is some form of conscious energy that is universal in nature and is without any specific form. However, it is immanent in all living and nonliving beings. It makes the universe vibrating with energy and activity.

Adi Shankaracharya, the great philosopher saint of India, was asked in his meeting with his guru who he was. To this he replied in a six-stanza composition called 'Nirvan Shatakam', which essentially says that 'I am not the body, not the mind nor the senses nor any material being. But I am the Pure Consciousness, eternal and infinite, that is present in all things and is the ultimate reality of the universe.' He was in fact referring to his core philosophy of 'Advait Vedanta,' the philosophy that he propagated through the length and breadth of the country with zeal and determination. Such spiritual effort is rarely in any religious literature.

Oneness of the whole creation has been stated very often in Hindu spiritual circles; in scriptures as well as in the writings and discourses of the saints. This is much emphasized in Vedanta as well. In fact, Vedanta comprises such features that could qualify it to be the universal religion.

Even in the early period of the Vedic era, it was accepted by the sages and common people that there is an ultimate prime force that drives the universe. It was considered the source and sink of all material things and beings. It was superior and above the nature-gods that were worshipped for various reasons. The Veda also states categorically that there is only one supreme reality and that the sages know it differently.

From scientific point of view, we know that the multiple forms of matter are also mere manifestations of energy. The ultimate reality is energy, or an energy field, and not matter as it appears to us. In that sense, our view is a false view. Shankaracharya also said that the world we see is not real. The basic material particle has been shown by science to be composed of vast amount of energy. This is the meaning of shanker's philosophy that terms the world an illusion. Further, all matter is formed of quarks, the quantum particles, which are mere packets of energy.

Again, there are four fundamental forces in the universe, the electromagnetic, the weak and strong nuclear forces and the force of gravity. Scientists are now engaged in research on a unified field theory that combines all the four forces. If there is one force that is the primary source of all these we again come to the concept of oneness in the universe. In simple terms, the debate between one and many existing simultaneously has been a long one and our scriptures stand testimony to it. I do hope one day, one reality will be accepted as the truth both by the spiritualists and the scientists.

When belief is tested over a period of time, it turns into faith. The sages found the truth by intuitive thought and meditation over long time. The science has taken the logical route that forms a theory and proves by experimentation. Finding truth is the goal for both. Let us hope they meet some day over the nature of Reality. That would certainly be a golden moment and a great achievement of human effort. Then science and spirituality would truly be united.

***

Some Thoughts for Consideration

Only those get the grace and blessings of the Supreme who have full faith in that. Pride is the basis of one's downfall. Do not feel proud of small achievement. It is a mistake to expect something from one whom you have helped. It only causes disappointment. Do every difficult task as the order of the Supreme. Surrender the fruit of that action to Supreme too. Never have the spirit of business with the Supreme. Everything is of the Supreme. You are only the caretaker for a while.

If you want to know something, then know your inner self. The rest is all a play of senses. If you want to kill somebody or something then kill the demon residing within you. If you want to win then win yourself. If you want to give something then give forgiveness and knowledge. If you want to take something then take blessings of others. If you want to distribute something then distribute happiness to all. If you want to fight, then fight for the country. If you want to run away from something, then run away from evil. If you want to have true love, then love the Supreme. If you want to control something or someone then control your anger. If you want to save something then save self-control and patience. These will come handy in times of difficulty. If you want to surrender, then do so to the Supreme. If you want to criticize someone then first look within you and be sure that you are clean yourself. Foul smell and foul behavior of others equally disturb us.

3
The Three Paths

It is one thing to stress the need of spirituality in our daily working life and quite another to actually do so. It requires a strong will and a conviction to follow a spiritual path. Religious scriptures provide us paths to follow. These paths are designed to suit the nature and personality of an individual.

Bhagwadgita provides us three paths. Though they are meant to achieve higher goal of uniting human consciousness to the pure consciousness, they work equally well to improve our spirituality in our daily life. The paths are suited as much to the intellectual as to the ordinary person who may be either too emotional in character or be a person believing in physical work for daily living.

The paths have been known as the path of knowledge, the path of devotional worship and the path of selfless work. Though the paths are different for different type of persons, each path leads to the same goal as it enlightens the person about the supreme power and how to unite our being with that. If followed with true spirit and full determination, it transforms even an evil being into a highly spiritual one. Hindu religious literature is replete with such cases.

These paths have been practiced for centuries and have found wide acceptability among the spiritual seekers. I introduce these paths in this chapter and take them again in later chapters for their relevance in building a balanced life.

3A. Devotion and Worship

It is common knowledge that to rise professionally, one must be devoted and sincere to his work. In the same way, to rise spiritually one must act sincerely in one's belief and worship of the Supreme Power. The prophets and sages have suggested various ways to do so. It is however true that one can be devoted to the Supreme without resorting to worship. But generally, it is common practice among some religions to show respect to the Supreme by reciting its name and indulge in rituals to please the all-powerful. Over the years, people have worshipped by creating images and idols of various forms in the name of their ideal or deity. Some people however, confine themselves to meditation alone as a path to connect with the Supreme. Personification of the Supreme Power is not without reason. The Supreme Power is behind every created being. Therefore, if you treat any being as the Supreme Power itself, logically you are right about doing so. But you must remember that any form you use you must view it as the real one. You must not quarrel over the difference in forms because all forms are manifestation of the same Supreme Power. Thus, multi-god worship is not wrong logically. It is justified on the basis of belief in the oneness of the whole universe. It is said that Supreme Power is formless and yet all forms are its own. That means the Supreme Power is immanent in all forms.

You cannot worship any being unless you have full faith in its representation of the Supreme. Therefore, faith is an important factor in the spiritual pursuit. Your spiritual growth depends on the intensity of your faith. The consequent results also depend on that. There is one other factor that is important in pursuing the path of devotional worship. Your mind must be cleaned of all the muck that this world puts in the form of egoistic actions in daily life. The part of pure consciousness in us is pure as snow but is surrounded by the dirt associated with our worldly actions. To see the brightness of this inner light we must remove the surrounding dirt by noble actions and right living.

One of the problems in learning is the attention deficit. This is commonly seen in many persons. Attention deficit means that one cannot focus one's mind over a matter for long. The mind wavers and changes gears from one subject to another rapidly. This hampers proper understanding and concentration. The problem is often seen early in children. it makes difficult for them to stay attentive and learn properly. It makes particularly difficult for them to learn subjects like mathematics which require a good attention span and concentration of mind.

Spiritual practice that requires concentration of mind on one object for a long period gives good result in improving attention span. It is a matter of practice and the result can be really satisfying for the practitioner.

Although the absolute Supreme Power is formless and is present everywhere it is not easy to make contact with that. To do that rituals are devised to turn our mind towards that power and thereby make a contact with that absolute one. We do so to convey our feelings and aspirations to that power. These rituals are meant to concentrate on this infinite and eternal reality and seek its help in our difficult and dire situations. This is done because we believe that this Supreme Power has infinite capacity to help us, help that no one in the world can provide us. Practically all religions have some rituals in one form or another because human feelings are common to most of us irrespective of our religion.

Worship and rituals are intimately connected. But we must remember that whenever we perform any ritual to connect us to the Supreme Power it is necessary to understand the reason and philosophy behind it. This will enable us to connect better, both emotionally and intellectually, and our action will be convincing and justified in our own mind. This brings in the intensity that is usually missing when we perform the ritual mechanically without involving our inner being into it.

There are some religious faiths that do not believe in any rituals and instead insist on only connecting mentally in meditation. That requires mental discipline of a high order. Most people lack that kind of discipline. Rituals therefore serve a purpose for most people to connect their body and mind to the Supreme Power and achieve their worldly purpose of seeking help from the Supreme one.

3B. Knowledge and Meditation

It is common knowledge that the spirit of enquiry and the desire to get knowledge about one's surroundings is natural to human beings. This has helped us to evolve better to the present state and has brought us to the commanding position compared to other species. This has enabled our brain to grow and made us an intelligent species. Meditation on the other hand, requires focus and single-minded attention on a specific object or a thought. At the same time, it is also said in our scriptures that meditation on the supreme reality makes us knowledgeable about the whole creation as it widens our consciousness to larger limits.

In the context of spirituality, knowledge and meditation provide a system of knowing and experiencing the Supreme Reality. It is a tradition of mysticism that has been practiced in the world, especially in the east, for several millennia. This practice has given to the world several persons of exceptional and extraordinary power. It is a quest for Self and finding the answer to the question 'who am I'.

Knowledge is necessary as a basic building block to strengthen one's faith in the Supreme Power, and then to experience the truth of that knowledge by spiritual practice such as the meditation. Knowledge about the Supreme has been gathered over the years by the record of experiences by the sages in the religious scriptures. The sages had a genuine desire to share their knowledge and experience with others. To that extent we owe a lot to them because they were indeed selfless in their efforts to enlighten the world.

Earlier it was done in the gurukul tradition in which a link was established between the teacher and the student like father and son. Slowly the tradition was weakened with time but still there are many institutions that awaken the inner light through genuine love for the seekers of truth. It must be emphasized here that for practicing meditation it is strongly advised to do it under the guidance of a guru.

Leading a balanced life implies that one must believe in being good and doing good in his or her worldly life even at the cost of personal loss. Everyone wants to be successful in life. But for doing so one must not leave his or her ideals. We generally depend upon our intellect to be successful in the worldly sense. But for right living, intellect alone is not enough. In fact intellect combined with bloated ego can make a person imbalanced in behavior. On the other hand, intellect alloyed with ethics and wisdom can take a person on the right path and also achieve success.

In spiritual circles, knowledge of Self is rated as the highest knowledge; even higher than any worldly knowledge. By the knowledge of Self, I mean the answer to the question 'who am I?' This subject is treated in depth in the Upanishads, the philosophical aspect of the Vedas.

There is a story about a young aspirant Nachiketa, the son of a sage, who is cursed to go to the god of death. When he meets the god of death after a long wait, he seeks the knowledge of Self from him. But the god of death tries to lure him to worldly wealth and other temptations instead. Nachiketa however, insists on getting the knowledge of Self. Ultimately god of death relents and describes him the secret of ultimate reality. He talks about the supreme reality of which we are a part and that is our true self.

Bhagwadgita gives us a summary of the Upanishad knowledge that is sacred to all Hindus. It is the philosophy of life that is both intellectual and practical. It serves to keep our spiritual aspect intact. This aspect keeps our working life on the right track by providing a balancing force to keep away negative tendencies, undesirable emotions and unwanted aspirations away from our thoughts.

Meditation is an essential part of our spiritual life. It is practiced by followers of most religious faiths since its aim is to establish contact with the Supreme Power and seek its energy for our worldly life. It makes us strong inwardly. It improves our working both emotionally and ethically. It makes us positive in outlook and enables us to experience our inner goodness that is our true nature. Meditation is not religion specific since it does not depend on any religious ritual. It makes us conscious of our inner light that ordinarily is covered by our negative thoughts and actions. Meditation, along with prayer to the 'Supreme', constitute Universal Religion since here the objective is to raise the very inner being of all humanity and create a balanced society that is just, kind, noble and loving.

Meditation now is a recognized way, worldwide, to heal and reduce stress for the overworked, and mentally stressed, persons. Its role in reducing tension, and thereby positively affecting both body and mind, is well appreciated by many persons irrespective of their religious affiliations. Medical science recognizes the effect of mind over body and many persons teach meditation techniques to relieve tension, stay calm and healthy in the present-day life of over work and intense competition. Yoga and meditation are now accepted practices for a healthy body and balanced mind in most countries of the world.

What started as a spiritual practice long ago has now become a practical solution to achieve a balanced life. It is particularly more important in the present age of technology where competition and for survival is a known fact.

In the Hindu faith, yoga and meditation have always been recognized as a way of life. This tradition has helped to them to be tolerant of other faiths and treat the whole world as one family. This mind set is all the more relevant and necessary in the present world where selfishness of individuals and that of nations is a fact of life. There is need to return ethics and morality in public life, and balancing the life of individuals through reasserting spirituality will go a long way in improving the situation and make the world a better place to live. Healthy body and mind are important to form a sane society. For this we have to reintroduce the spiritual component in our daily life.

3C. Selfless Work

Work and action are important not only for our survival but also to keep our body and mind in good health. We work for our living; we study for getting ideas and we take action whenever our life id in jeopardy or in danger of getting harmed. Practically every person has to work for food, clothing and shelter, barring of course those who are blessed with inherited wealth. We work for our good and also to harm others in revenge. We act in anger, jealousy and hatred as also out of love for others, to help the needy, the poor and the helpless. Thus, we keep working all our life, to do work that is sometime good, sometime not so good.

All this work has repercussions on our future. It is therefore truly said that we make our destiny by the kind of work we did in the past and the work that we do in the present. In general, our work defines our personality and our place in society. How should we work so that it includes the spiritual aspect also in our daily life? This question has been very well answered in the Bhagwadgita where it is stated that we must perform our duty, and do other work that is necessary for our survival and growth, but never feel disheartened when it does not bring the result to our expectation or when we fail to get the reward for our hard work. We can also interpret it in another way; namely, we must be dispassionate enough to face the consequences of our efforts without getting discouraged or disheartened. To do work is in our hands but to get the desired result there are many other factors or forces that are out of our control.

In simple and literal terms, selfless work implies that you have the right to work and action but not on the fruit of it. On the face of it, it is a simple statement but it has deep implications on the working life of an individual. It spiritualizes the person by its practice since it reduces the egoistic attachment to our self-oriented activities. It puts faith in the will of the Supreme Power.

This way of working is a sort of detachment with self-oriented activities which are necessary but bring disappointment in reward. Work we must do, but we should remain calm and balanced in reaction, emotional or otherwise, if success eludes us. Circumstances under which we work are equally important in affecting the result. The unexpected happenings, the nature's mood, the effect of past activities and others' involvement, all of these determine the end result of our actions. This however, certainly does not mean that we should stop making earnest efforts to succeed. It only means we should not be sad or disheartened in failure but take the result philosophically and leave it to the will of the 'Supreme Power.

In the matter of result of our effort, submission of our will to that of the Supreme is seen in some other faiths too but Bhagwadgita makes a special case for it and advocates it as a way of life. This is the way of selfless work. It is prescribed as the practical way, the right way, to perform our duties. It is one of the three ways to bring spirituality in our practical life. It reduces our ego because more the ego more the hurt in failure. In this sense it brings some commonality between three paths since reduction of ego is a characteristic feature of spiritual behavior. Selfless work therefore, trains our mind to have equality, tolerance, and acceptance of the inevitable. It builds a bond with the Supreme by subjugating our will to that of the Supreme. It leads to a frame of mind that does not get disturbed over failures and remains calm and balanced under all situations. It removes anger and frustration when we do not get what we desire. It makes us accept the power of the Supreme humbly and thereby learn a lesson of life.

Every failure has a lesson for us. Our inborn desires are so strong that we fail to see the hidden lesson and start blaming others or our fate for our failures. We forget that we ourselves make our destiny by our past and present activities and the Supreme Power is not to be blamed for this. We blame that Power for going against us but that is the result of our ignorance. We neglect ethics and spirituality in our actions and then we expect to be forgiven by nature for our faults and selfishness.

Selfless work is a sure remedy for reducing and controlling undesirable emotions and unnecessary aspirations from our thinking. This helps in avoiding pitfalls in our daily work.

As said earlier, failure hurts ego as we all know by experience; the more the ego, the greater the pain and frustration. Selfless work makes us equanimous in such situations. It thereby reduces our ego. It is a step towards bringing in spiritual outlook in our work and behavior. Ego is behind many of our wrong actions. Spiritual advice tells us to love and not do any harm to others. Ego is good to the extent that it helps to be competitive. But excessive ego harms in many ways. Selfless action trains us to remain same in both success and failure. It brings wisdom in daily behavior. In a sense, selfless work is a spiritual practice that takes us to a higher level of consciousness in which we develop dispassion, control negative emotions and do not harm others for personal gain and so on.

For men and women of present age, selfless work is an easy, and yet very potent, tool to bring spirituality in our life and thereby lead a balanced life. It does not need knowledge of high order nor rigorous religious rituals. It does not even need long pours of spiritual training under a master. The spirit of selflessness is a great reducer of ego. It brings equality and love for all in the chaotic world of selfish tendencies and personal gain at the cost of others.

***

The Good Ones and Not ao Good Ones

Some live with ideals while some others live without any direction or aim. Someone's life is a source of pleasure while someone else's life is a source of misery to others. Someone shows right path to others while some other deviates others purposely.

Someone shows the light in the path of life while someone else creates darkness. Somebody, on the strength of his personality spreads love while another one seeds hatred. Someone becomes a compassionate co-traveler while another one deceives and steals. Someone in his talk creates merely noise while another one in his silence imparts knowledge. Someone is happy by troubling others while another becomes happy by forgiving the wrong doer. Someone in his desire to earn money does a sinful act while another earns blessing of others by donating wealth. Somebody dies in protecting the honor of the country while another one does not hesitate to betray the country. Someone keeps asking for boons from the Supreme one while another one surrenders everything to that. Someone earns fame by being kind while another one makes himself pitiful by his action.

4
Prayer

It is human nature to seek favor from the powerful. We do so from the boss, from the political leader and from the rich as well. When we learn from spiritual sources that the Supreme Power is all-powerful, prayer to that comes naturally to us. It is also a fact that most of us suffer difficulty in our life on account of health, finance, and revengeful action of others and so on. We feel utterly helpless in such situations and resort to prayer to the Supreme one. Temples, mosques, gurudwaras and churches are testimony to that.

We also know that our prayer is answered when we pure at heart, full of faith and humble in request. These are spiritual qualities. Prayer therefore, is a part of spirituality. It is however a strange fact that some people with evil in them pray for harming others. But that is not spiritual. Good intention is an important factor in the success of prayer. Prayer for selfish ends is generally more common among people than otherwise.

The sages of Vedic era have always stressed that prayer must be for the general good of the whole humanity. Most Vedic prayers are in that spirit. It is rightly said that when you pray for all you are inevitably included in that. It is a thought worth considering by those who generally pray for themselves or for their near and dear ones alone.

Prayer can be done silently or aloud depending upon the preference of the individual. But in my view prayer in silence is preferable since it gives better concentration on the Supreme.

Should we pray only when we are in difficulty? In this connection we must remember an advice from a saint. It says everybody remembers the Supreme when one is in trouble or having a bad time, but nobody remembers when one is having a good time. If one remembered even in pleasant or good time, then why would one be in trouble or have a bad time?' The message is clear. Be regular in prayer. It should be made a habit. Whether you do it once a day or twice a day that is your choice, but doing it regularly has its own merit. If you are interested in spiritual practice then it is imperative to be regular in doing so. Those who practice meditation also start their meditation with a prayer. Those who believe in the worship of their deity, they do it after their worship. The whole idea is to show one's respect to the Supreme Power and feel humble before it. They also seek the blessings of the Supreme to get success in their spiritual effort.

Those who are under the tutelage or the discipleship of a guru or a spiritual master, dead or alive, they include in the prayer a humble request seeking their blessings too. This is because they consider the guru or the master an embodiment of the Supreme and therefore give him the same respect as the Supreme Power.

Mass prayer has more potency than that of a single person. Many spiritual teachers insist on this for its better efficacy. This is true for mass meditation too.

Let me take an example of a prayer that seeks well of all. The Vedic prayers are generally of this nature. One such prayer says: O Supreme one, take us from untruth to truth; from darkness to light and from death to immortality. On the face of it, it looks simple enough, but it has deeper meaning also. Going from untruth to truth may mean a simple ethical advice but in reality, it means going from worldly living in falsehood to the absolute truth of the Supreme one. The Supreme one is the only truth since it is eternal and always exists. Everything else is unreal or untrue since it exists only for a finite time. Only the eternal is true the rest is false.

The second part is easier to understand. Here darkness and light signify ignorance and knowledge respectively. So, the sage is asking for the knowledge of the Self for all. According to the Vedic belief salvation or freedom from the cycle of birth and death is not possible without the knowledge of the Self. Most people live without this knowledge and hence they are living in darkness. It is a prayer to raise the level of human consciousness to the Supreme consciousness.

The third part is more significant. Death refers to the fact that everything that is born must die. That is the law of nature. So, death is the end of every one of us. But everybody wants to live forever. In other words, every one seeks immortality. But in the physical world immortality is impossible since all matter must decay in nature. Immortality here refers to the situation where human consciousness merges with the eternal Super consciousness. That is the way to immortality.

Thus, the whole prayer seeks salvation or immortality for all through the knowledge of Self. The sage is seeking this through the kind help of the Supreme Power. This is the type of prayer that takes us to the path of spirituality and enables human consciousness to rise to higher levels of divine existence.

Let me now give an example of a prayer that most of us worldly people would like to recite. It has no philosophical overtones and is quite mundane in nature. It goes like this:

O Supreme one, you are infinite, eternal, all-powerful, all-knowing, all-seeing, all-pervading and present in all beings. Let everyone have happy and pleasant life, good health and enough resources for our daily needs. Let your grace shine on us always. Make us follow the path of righteous living and loving relationships. Give us wisdom enough to be kind and charitable to all and not harm anybody out of revenge or vengeance. Let our hearts be pure and our minds be inclined always to your remembrance. Have mercy on all humanity and forgive our undesirable acts and negative tendencies, for we know not what we do out of ignorance. Let us all be positive in outlook and shun negativity. We bow to you in reverence and humility and seek your blessings in everyday life.

Here is another one of a different kind:

O Supreme one, you are the cause and the foundation of this material world. You are the very energy that gives meaning and movement to this universe. You are infinite and eternal. You are the force behind our senses, our thoughts and our actions. You are the mind and energy of this visible and invisible universe. You are the light in the stars. You are the mysterious seed that created the universe. You are the past, present and future of this creation. O Supreme one, give us the wisdom to appreciate your presence within us and remember you every moment till we die.

***

Who Created Evil in the World?

A frustrated man once went to a swami and asked in a complaining voice, 'Sir, why did God create so much evil in this world? Due to this evil life has become so difficult and full of suffering.' The swami smiled and said.' My dear fellow, who told you God created evil in this world. It was not He but MAN who created evil out of his actions. God had given him a heaven like earth and a wonderful gift of highly competent brain with a free will to act as he liked. But the man misused his brain and freedom of action and created hell on this earth. it was man who cheated, looted and robbed others in self-interest. It was he only who deceived, bribed, hated, envied and misappropriated the goodwill of others. It was man again who, out of greed, spoiled the environment and acted cruelly towards other species. God gave fresh air, sweet water and fruit trees. He even tolerated the wrong doings of man and sustained the environment for healthy living. But man broke His trust and kept on doing all the wrong things just to outsmart and hoodwink his fellow beings. Then God made a rule. Whatever man did he will have to bear the result of his actions. Now that rule applies and man suffers. Strangely, man blames God for his sufferings. Now tell me is it God who is to be blamed for evil and suffering in this world?'

The frustrated man kept mum and did not reply.

5
FIVE LEVELS

spiritual

intuition

higher mind

lower mind

body and life

Fig. 1 five levels of existence

In the above figure are shown five levels [or sheaths, as mentioned in Upanishad] through which human consciousness has to pass, and reject, before it reaches the highest level of enlightenment and sees the inner light. Each level or sheath has to be peeled off by spiritual effort that requires mental discipline and sustained practice of spirituality, preferably under the guidance of a guru.

The first level refers to body and life. It is actually two levels which mean body centered and vitality. Body centered means the person's thoughts and actions are most of the time concerned with his/her body. The person is either too much interested in food related matters or is most of the time thinking of how to improve or beautify his/her body. Activities like body building, playing games, interest in outdoor sports, gymnastics or athletics are all concerned with body or vitality. If one concentrates on these matters most of the time then his/her consciousness remains preoccupied with such matters and there is little chance of the person to go for higher aims of spirituality. Of course, there are many persons who spend their life at this level of existence. At the same time, one has to appreciate that body and vitality are the basis of our existence. There is nothing good or bad about it. It only means that if you are interested in raising your existence level to higher aims you have to make an effort to do so by finding time for it and bring about a change in your way of life.

The next level is that of lower mind. It concerns the engagement of mind in daily activities for supporting life. It means activities related to sense inputs and reactions to emotions as well as activities for earning livelihood. Here one is not concerned with higher aims of life or intellectual involvement of high order. Here too if one is interested in spiritual pursuit one has to make effort to change one's way of life and get started towards spiritual activity. It must be noted that majority of people in the world remain at this level since it is related to their very existence.

The next level is the level of intellect. At this level, intellectuals live with ideas that can change the world. They may be scientists, philosophers, artists of high caliber and even leaders of masses who make a change in the way people live. They think high and act high. Their consciousness rests in higher mind. They have an aim in life and they act to achieve that. They can move to spirituality through acquiring of knowledge of Self if their curiosity about the reality of nature interests them. They are not bound by traditional way of life and make their own way that interests them. But in any society their number is small.

The dotted line separates the material living from the purely spiritual or the divine domain of the Supreme. The spiritual domain has many sub levels depending on the spiritual attainment of the person. The lowest of these sub levels of the divine is the level of intuition. The highest of these levels is the level of merging one's consciousness with the Supreme consciousness or seeing the inner light. At this merger, the person becomes universal in outlook and his consciousness spreads to all humanity.

The spiritual aim is to rise from the lowest level to the highest. For this one has to raise one's consciousness in stages. We know most people are at the stage of lower mind. To go from this stage to the spiritual domain one method is to use one's emotions to cross over the dotted line through devotional worship. This is the method employed by the saints who worship their deity with full emotional involvement by worshipping daily and focusing their thoughts wholeheartedly on that. The other method is to acquire enough knowledge about the Supreme through their intellect and then focus on knowing oneself. They use logic to find out through the answer to the question 'who am I? 'This is the method that many great spiritual masters have adopted.

Acquiring intuition by spiritual practice is the sign that you are moving on the right path since intuition is the first step on the ladder to spiritual success. As you move further on the other higher levels of spiritual domain, signs become visible through acquiring other powers. The guru knows the steps of progress and leads you further on the path.

For ordinary worldly people who have a family and have to perform various functions to run the family, it is too ambitious to aim for the highest state of spirituality. It is enough if they can just cross over the dotted line and enter spiritual domain. This will bring a balance in their worldly life. They will then see ethics and morality taking an important role in their daily behavior. They may not become saints exactly but a marked change will appear in their whole personality. This is what is required in the present age of stressful life. That is why I suggest that spiritual content must be added to our daily routine so that we become better in our own interest and in the interest of all others.

***

Supreme Consciousness

This is the highest state of consciousness that a seeker of spirituality reaches as a reward to his quest for knowing the reality of existence. This is the realization of a liberated or enlightened person in the highest state of meditation on the Supreme. To reach this state some suggest that you unlearn your worldly experiences while others say that you meditate on an object and then eventually reach the state of no thought or complete riddance of ego. For all seekers of spirituality, the goal is the same but the paths are different. This is the state of being in super consciousness, devoid of any conditioning of the mind. The mind gets conditioned due to our preferences and prejudices. Great yogis and saints reach this state after rigorous mental discipline practiced by concentrating on the Supreme. When the spiritual seeker reaches this state of supreme consciousness, his/her human consciousness merges with super consciousness and the person becomes universal in outlook and one with Supreme.

Our worldly experiences lead to various levels of egoism. The salvation lies in reducing ego that is a hurdle in the growth of spirituality. In doing so there is no need to unduly repress or suppress the undesirable emotions. This suppression may lead to a pathological state of mind that is regressive to the practice of spirituality. This unconditioned supreme consciousness is one with the supreme power, the only reality of existence, it is as mysterious as mystery can be. It is invisible and yet present everywhere and within us. It is nameless and formless and yet people give different names to it. It is called Brahman, God, Super consciousness and inner light. But none is easily comprehensible to a common man untrained in spirituality. It is the creator of mind and matter. It is beyond intellect and logic and yet it creates and sustains everything seen or unseen. it is infinite and eternal, the source and sink of all beings and things. It is both manifested and un-manifested, the be all and end all.

6
Head and Heart

Both our head and heart contribute to the growth of spirituality. We can learn about the Supreme through scriptures and gather knowledge about various spiritual activities that help us to achieve our objective. There is enormous amount of literature on the subject. We have already stated earlier that knowledge and meditation is a time-tested path for attaining the goal, though a bit more difficult than some other paths. Head provides us the faculty of discrimination to judge what is right and what is wrong for us. Through the use of intellect, we can filter the information that pours on us all the time. Through intellect we can aim high in our life and not be content with mundane affairs of the world. It gives us a purpose and the way to achieve that.

We connect our emotions with our heart. It is the storehouse of our feelings like love, kindness, brotherhood, sharing and so on. We feel love for the Supreme through our heart. This is an essential requirement for spiritualizing us through devotion and worship. Love for the mankind is also a spiritual quality. It is our heart that intuitively accepts ethical values and rejects the negative feelings of hatred, jealousy, deceit and so on. Purity of heart is absolutely essential before one starts on the path of meditation and inward journey.

Both head and heart have a role in developing and strengthening faith. Emotion is not the only thing that gives us faith. Faith based on emotion alone may not last long since emotions change with time and circumstances. It needs the conviction derived from knowledge, reason and convincing arguments to retain belief and faith. Because it is necessary to sustain belief in the Supreme for the growth of spirituality, we need both the faculties of head and heart in the pursuit of spiritual attainment. It is the head that separates superstition from spirituality. Even in the practice of spirituality, we need a healthy head to learn the procedures and practices for cleaning our mind and body. We need knowledge from the records of experiences of sages and deliberate on them.

It is my experience that merely from reading spiritual literature for a long time you will notice a change in your thinking pattern and behavior towards others, provided of course you do it with faith and perseverance. Every input that goes to your brain generates an effect in your psychological system. Therefore, both good and not so good audio-visual input has its influence on your thoughts and deeds. To avoid negative influence, you have to make special efforts to counter negativity.

We all know about the good and bad influence on our children by their friends; the more vulnerable they are, the greater the effect. For practitioners of spirituality, it is considered advisable to read and listen to the spiritual texts on a regular basis. This is common in most organized institutions, which teach, preach and train people for a spiritual way of life.

The head also has a role in removing negative tendencies and harmful emotions from our mind. It is suggested by a spiritual guru that one must read at least five pages of spiritual literature daily and / or listen to good classical music or see a good painting. These are creations of those whose consciousness ordinarily resides in the domain of higher mind. Such activities on the part of seeker of spirituality inspire him/her to a higher aim in life. This takes our thinking a step higher and additionally relieves us of the stress caused by mundane problems.

In chapter 5 we have seen that one can cross over to the spiritual domain either through knowledge (higher mind) or through emotional devotion and worship (lower mind). This indicates that both head and heart are equally important in reaching the spiritual domain. However, one must remember that merely knowing the Supreme is not enough. One must experience it in order to be truly enlightened. That is why spiritual knowledge must be supplemented by meditation to have direct experience of the Supreme. In devotion and worship, the path being emotional, the psychic experience comes naturally to the seeker.

It is common knowledge that connecting with the Supreme Power is a matter of experience to the individual. One person's experience may differ from that of another, but it is the experience that enlightens the seeker.

When we pray, again it is both head and heart that contribute to the praying activity. The words originate from the head but the emotion comes from the heart. Therefore, the role of one or the other cannot be underestimated. When I say this, I am aware that it applies to many spiritual activities. But there have been cases where totally illiterate persons have attained great spiritual heights. In such cases, the intensity of emotion is so high that it overpowers all other thinking and the person becomes single-mindedly devoted to the object of his attention, the image or the idol of his deity. The emotion in this case is generally that of love. In most cases, this is an overpowering emotion that takes control of the person's whole thinking mechanism

In the context of present-day seekers of spirituality, we know that most of them are leading their life with intellect and emotions. Intellect is necessary to sail through the sea of life. We have gadgets and devices that need some intellect to operate. Without familiarity with these gadgets, it is not possible to go through daily activities. Therefore, these days, ignoring the head is not possible. The practice of spirituality must take account of this fact of life.

***

Some Thoughts for Consideration

Our mind shuts off the inner light from our perception just like the moon shuts off the sunlight on eclipse. The mind becomes silent in meditation. Then the obstruction vanishes and the inner light shines forth.

We live in a world of various levels of reality; from gross state to the subtle state. In this changing state of reality, the only thing that is permanent and without change is the pure consciousness. This Supreme consciousness is the true reality of existence.

Money or wealth is a convenience, though necessary, for living in this world. Let it remain within its limits. Do not make it the aim of life.

Pass through the shining street of this world but do not get dazzled by its brilliant temptations that may stop your walk to the goal.

It is better to be good than great.

Do not let your desires be so overpowering that they make you forget the aim of life.

Life is an experience. Learn from it as much as you can.

Do not snatch others life to make your life better.

Life is a river. Its water has come from the sea and it will go the sea. Do not let the stones on the way stop its flow.

Do not look behind nor worry about what is ahead. Keep moving.

To ape others is the habit of monkey. Man has evolved much ahead from its predecessor. Do not lose your self- identity in aping others.

Values of life are invaluable. Do not lose them

Before you act, always decide what is right and what is wrong.

Never forget the Supreme Power. It is the only truth of this universe. That is ever living and never changing. Everyone's identity is because of that.

Never feel alone in times of difficulty. The Supreme one is always with you. Moreover, time never stays the same forever.

7
ETHICS AND SPIRITUALITY

From very early times, ethics and morality have been inseparable part of spirituality. Early sages understood the importance of these for a stable society and included them as necessary norms for daily life. Anyone who wished to follow the spiritual path was told to improve one's personal and social behavior first and refrain from negative tendencies that acted as obstructions in the path. It was considered wrong to acquire spiritual powers without first being ethically and morally correct. However, considering the human nature, there have been still some persons who prayed and worshipped the Supreme Being for success in their nefarious activities. We have heard about dacoits worshipping their deity before going to rob innocent people. No one would like to call such persons as spiritual or religious. Even these days, we find people doing prayers and worship in temples and then indulging in cheating, deceiving and harming others in many ways. These people only wear a cloak of spirituality or religiosity but are neither spiritual nor religious in the right sense.

Early philosophers, great thinkers, saints and sages laid down certain norms for people to follow for right living. This was in the interest of a society that was healthy, moral, socially cohesive, and peace loving. Those who had the high aim of spiritual union with the Supreme, this acted as the basic ground to start with, in order to walk on the path of salvation.

Ethics and morality are necessary for a spiritual seeker in more ways than one. It not only brings purity in mind and body but also helps in the practice and growth of spirituality. The spiritual progress is much faster for a person of ethical and moral conduct.

Ethical and moral living has always been a part of spiritual practice. Long ago, the great sage Patanjali, who wrote a treatise on the method of achieving salvation through yoga and meditation, included ethics and morality as the first steps in his eight-fold method. He enumerated and explained the things one must do and not do under two heads. Each head carried five such imperatives. He emphasized that these ten imperatives be made a part of life if the seeker of salvation wanted to achieve the goal.

Briefly, the eight-fold method contains eight steps; ethical and moral living, physical postures for healthy living, breath control, inward drawing of senses, concentration of mind on an object for short and long time and finally absorption of self in the Supreme Reality and stay in the supreme consciousness.

Although the two groups of five imperatives each are mentioned in connection with the achievement of higher aim of self-absorption in the Supreme one, they are equally valid in the modern context of right living. Most people are interested in avoiding suffering in their lives. Very few are concerned with salvation. Right living with ethical and moral principles is a step in the direction of achieving a life that is either free of suffering or has less suffering than it would be otherwise. This is because our actions make our destiny and right living avoids wrong actions because of proper mental training.

The eight-fold method also has the general objective of avoiding suffering, though the main objective of sage Patanjali was the attainment of salvation through yoga and meditation. By salvation we mean absorption of self in the Supreme. Effectively it means raising our consciousness to the level of supreme consciousness. Yoga literally means joining or merging of self with the Supreme Being. This is the real aim, and true meaning, of the eight-fold method. But popularly, throughout the world, the word yoga has come to mean the physical postures that give relief from ailments and keep one healthy by their daily practice. These postures form only a part of the eight-fold method of sage Patanjali.

The lofty aim of salvation may be too farfetched for an ordinary person in the present world. But raising the level of our spiritual quotient certainly helps to reduce our suffering. This modest objective is quite achievable, and hence desirable, to be tried through righteous living that has a touch of spirituality.

The first set of five points that needs strict following in the eight-fold method are the abstinences. They are; (i) nonviolence, (ii) truthfulness (iii) non-stealing (iv) chastity (v) non--avarice. These are essentially ethical rules.

Nonviolence has been always important in Hindu way of life. It essentially means non-injury to others, physical or mental. In the larger context it means that your living should not harm any other being in any way. It has also been stated elsewhere as live and let live. It follows the principle of nature that you have as much right on this planet as any other. Killing another for your selfish reason is just not right. When you have no power to give life you have no right to snatch it away either. Some other religions like Buddhism and Jainism also support nonviolence in letter and spirit.

Truthfulness is recognized as a good quality throughout the world by all the religious followers. Even if some of those who follow no religion, it is accepted by them that speaking truth is a necessary thing. Courts insist on this. Priests advise this. The philosophers assume that truth is important. Scientists believe in discovering the truth. Saints and sages spend their life in the pursuit of truth behind existence. Every society hate lies and falsehood. And yet, very few people in worldly life stick to it. The reason of course is self-interest. Therefore, speaking truth always is possible only if you rise above yourself. That is why it is made mandatory for those who aspire to follow the spiritual way of life. People's belief is won only by those who stick to truthfulness. A liar can never win the confidence of others.

Non-stealing implies that you live within your means and do not usurp the earnings of others. Do not try to get what is not yours. Stealing, snatching, and robbing are unworthy of a right living person. Taking others' rightful possession by force or by deceit is a recognized crime. This is accepted by all those whose job is to dispense justice. The habit of stealing is a mental aberration. Such persons are unfit to follow the path of spirituality. Unrightfully possessing something is certainly not right for a right living person.

Chastity in a broad sense implies sexual restraint and not total abstinence of sex. For a worldly person it means marital fidelity and avoiding adultery. But in the present world, sexual norms and practices differ a lot from region to region, country to country and religion to religion. Conservative people have a different take on this compared to so called advanced civilizations. For example, adultery may be a crime in one national or geographical group but not in another. But restraint in sexual matters is advisable for all; certainly, for those who desire to live right with some element of faith in spiritual way of life. As I said before, most people are interested in leading a worldly life and not become a monk or a saint. Their level of spirituality is limited to some kind of faith in the Supreme Being and to seek His blessings for a trouble-free life. For them any advice for avoidance of sex would be an impractical proposition.

In olden times, the original Sanskrit word for avoiding sexual relations meant celibacy. But it was for those who opted for lifetime meditation in jungles to obtain salvation. They were totally cut off from the mainstream worldly life. Their aim was the highest achievement of self-absorption in the Supreme Being. However, in modern worldly life this aim is too high for most people. For these therefore, chastity in family life is a better option, which incidentally is a practical one too.

Non-avarice implies avoiding extreme greed for wealth or material gain. This is quite important for seekers of spirituality in the present age. It means do take steps to earn your living and provide for your family but do not indulge in acquisitions that only go to feed your greed. One must clearly distinguish between need and greed. Greed for too many possessions takes you away from spiritual path, even though your spiritual goal may be a modest one. Greed is a negative tendency that has adverse consequences. One must remember that one is truly a temporary custodian of wealth. All real wealth remains with nature and it only changes its owner from time to time. It applied to your ancestors as much as it applies to you. For centuries the landed property has passed on from father to son and never remained with one person for long. The conquered land by the kings has become people's property now and passed on to private hands. When there is no permanent possession why worry then about its greedy possession.

The whole point about the above five abstinences is not to create extraneous thoughts in the mind that take away your away from the spiritual aim of right living.

The second group of five points that need to be observed rigorously by the seeker of spirituality in personal life include (i) purity of mind, speech and body (ii) contentment (iii) self-discipline (iv) self-study and (v) contemplation of the Supreme Being.

Purity of mind is of utmost importance in the spiritual pursuit. It is commonly known that a dirty mind brings trouble for all while a pure mind not only improves self but does good to others as well. The brain gets inputs from the senses that directly or indirectly affect the thought process. It is therefore important that we see or hear only that which is good for us and forget or neglect that can affect us badly. Our reading and viewing should avoid dirty stuff that can go to our memory and ultimately descend to the subconscious. Such matter resurfaces to our mind involuntarily at times and makes our mental processes impure. The audiovisual input in childhood has a lot of influence in our adult mental make- up. Even in adulthood, what we see or hear from different sources can change our behavior adversely if we are not careful. There are many agencies that put out undesirable stuff in visual and print media to earn money. But it is for us to respond to that stuff with responsibility and understanding rather than absorb that muck to our disadvantage. In this connection remember that famous three -monkeys' image that says see no evil, speak no evil and hear no evil. This brings purity in speech on equal ground in importance with other inputs to our senses. We must also note that only pure mind can harbor pure thoughts and sustain faith in the Supreme Being.

Purity in speech implies that we must keep our language free from abuses, hateful words and any indication of annoyance or anger. Our speech defines our mental personality. We get respect when our speech shows knowledge and respect for others' views. Some people develop the habit of punctuating their speech with dirty abuses. These abusive words have no relevance to the substance, nor do they add anything to the information content. Such persons only bring disrespect in the mind of the listener. One may well ask why purity in speech is important for spirituality. The simple reason is that words reflect your thoughts. Improper words show improper training of the mind.

Purity of body generally refers to the cleanliness and hygienic maintenance of your body. It is obviously meant to maintain good health for pursuing the goal of spiritual attainment. Living under impure and unclean environment is detrimental both for health as well as high thinking. Simple but clean living, in body and mind, is an important requirement for pursuing higher goals. Spending unnecessary time on improving physical looks has no spiritual benefit. On the other hand, this time could be usefully employed in practicing spiritual techniques that would raise your consciousness to a higher level. This applies equally to both genders, though opinion on this may differ depending on the way people want to live, and the views they may have on the need of including spirituality in our way of life. I say this because practice of spirituality and training of mind takes time to mature and become fruitful for right living.

Contentment gives peace of mind. It provides freedom from unnecessary worry about lack of this and that. This leads to a healthy mind. A healthy mind is capable of thinking right. Thus, it is necessary to remain calm and contented if you intend to follow the path of spirituality and right living. Dissatisfaction leads to tension of one kind or another. Tension is responsible for bad health, physical and mental.

Contentment does not only refer to satisfaction about what you have and not worry about lack of wealth and prosperity. It also means acceptance of others high profile living and not feel jealous about it. It is an acceptance of one's circumstances as they are. However, it is not a defeatist attitude. It does not make one unwilling to do better. It only means not to get disturbed and become worrisome and waste time in blaming oneself for not becoming like others. It allows one to remain optimistic about one's capabilities and yet not run after getting things that are not really necessary for our living right. As I said before, money and wealth are good up to a point. One need not become a slave to one's desire to acquire more and more. Developing a craze to get more and more, only takes you away from higher goals of life that have nothing to do with material possession or material gain. Spiritual growth is one such area where material prosperity of high order is of no help. A contented person is better prepared to concentrate his//her mind on meditation. It is because extraneous thoughts about worldly possessions do not clutter his/her mind. The spirit of contentment also applies to other areas where you compare yourself with others in competing with the, because all disappointments and worries only keep your mind disturbed and make it unfit for concentration and meditation. A contented mind is a restful mind.

Self-discipline is required to practice spirituality with persistence and perseverance. One needs such discipline that is often found among those who practice austerity and asceticism in their life. Following the path of meditation for self-absorption in the Supreme Being is not an easy task. It requires extreme dedication and hard work. That is why for such objective this kind of discipline is demanded from the seeker of salvation. One is reminded about the difficult postures and long years of meditation by the yogis for this purpose. But for those who wish to practice spirituality in the present age, leading a worldly life with family and friends, one need not go for such austere and ascetic ways for modest objective of right living. All that is necessary is to put oneself under sufficient self-control and self-discipline so that a consistency is maintained in pursuing the practice of prayer, meditation and daily remembrance of the Supreme Being. In doing so, keep the mind and body pure and clean. Also, do not entertain extraneous thoughts that take you away from the object of meditation. All this requires some sort of self-discipline in maintaining continuity, persistence and perseverance. This point is stressed because in the busy life of present-day worldly people, who have to work hard to make a living, time is important. Shortage of time should not become a reason to discontinue what you start with the aim of improving your lifestyle with right living.

Self-study includes study of spiritual literature as well as study of self. This means gathering of knowledge about the Supreme as well as finding the true reality of one self. When you do that, you find the same conclusion, namely our true self is the supreme reality and none else. The initiation into spiritual path starts with the study of Vedas for Hindus and prime religious books for persons of other faiths. This study gives the necessary faith into the path of spirituality. The other texts by great sages, saints and religious teachers of eminence provide the necessary confidence in moving ahead on the path of spiritual growth. The spiritual knowledge has an important role in shaping our spiritual outlook towards life.

Moving inwards, turning senses from outward to inwards, and meditating on the Supreme One, gives practical experience of the Supreme power through meditation. It gives an experience that is subject specific but, in all cases, provides peace of mind, serenity and tranquility.

Self-study also includes self-reflection, and introspection of self's thoughts, speech and actions. This is a very important part of inward movement of the spiritual seeker. The method of knowledge lays great stress on this aspect.

Contemplation of the Supreme Being is necessarily important in meditation. The Supreme Being is given various names that are all synonyms of the same power. We say Brahman, True Self or simply Self, unchanging reality, Supreme One, Supreme consciousness, Super consciousness, Cosmic consciousness and so on. These synonyms are often used for what is popularly known as God. Effectively however, it is the power that is behind all creation, sustenance and destruction of the whole universe. This power is idolized, prayed to, or worshipped in personalized form also. Some people however prefer to talk of this as formless, infinite and eternal force that is largely unknown in strict sense. Some religions simply call it God and leave it at that without defining it any further

The above ten points, two sets of five points each, enable us to have personal growth with ethical, moral, and spiritual content. In this way, they help us to live a balanced life in thoughts, words and deeds. This should be the prime objective of our life in this world. That includes the interest of ever body, including ourselves, for right living.

***

Who is the Best?

Once there was a contest going for the award of a trophy to the best person of the year. The contest was arranged by a private organization. For this award, there were a number of contestants from different fields of specialization. There were scientists, military officials, sports persons, artists and lawyers. There were some social scientists too and some political leaders. They all had made a name for themselves and were highly regarded for their achievements. The contestants were given fifteen minutes each to present their work and describe their contribution to their field of work. Each praised his/her work sky high with pride and a sense of glory.

But in the end the jury failed to decide on any name. the decision was then left to the chairman of the jury. Somehow the chairman also could not come to any definite conclusion because everyone had done the best in their respective field during the year. Seeing the indecision on the face of the chairman, a lean old man in the jury, approached the chairman and said,' please decide on the merit of that person who has not only made a mark for himself/herself in his/her field of specialization but also has cultivated humanistic approach and benefited the maximum number of people by his/her work.' His argument was that humanism and benefit to people was any day better than the self-achievement of a person. The chairman liked the suggestion, and gave another ten minutes each to the contestants to describe the benefit their work had accrued to the people at large. This enabled the chairman to make the decision.

In spirituality also, it is not only necessary to improve yourself but also benefit the society by your self- achievement. In a way, it already does so, to some extent, since your balanced life and good behavior does well to others and it improves the social environment.

8
Tendencies and Emotions

So far, we have talked about the abstinences and observances to be followed in our daily life in order to prepare ourselves for a spiritual and ethical life. These qualities are necessary to make us fit for spiritual practices and move on to the path of right living successfully. But there are certain tendencies and emotions that also play their part in our physical and mental behavior and actions. They also need to be put under proper management to bring out our best in life. For example, we have not said anything about anger or love, which give strong reactions from any person to whom they may be aimed at. Similarly, there are other negative and positive aspects of our personality that need to be corrected in order to make us move on the right path and live a balanced life. Some of these are hatred, jealousy, ego, anger, tendency to dominate in unhealthy competition, criticizing and back-biting others for no particular reason. And then there are some positive emotions that need to be cultivated such as love, compassion, empathy, forgiveness, charity, dispassion, discrimination between good and bad, real/unreal, and surrender to the Supreme Being etc. it may be an uphill task to succeed in all of these efforts to improve but one can certainly try as much as possible. I know nobody is perfect, nor one can achieve perfection in a short span of a few years. But life is all about try, and trying hard to improve as much as one can do in one life.

Hating someone is an expression of negativity within us. It is unspiritual in the sense spiritual person believes that the Supreme Being resides in every heart and therefore hating someone amounts to hating the Supreme one itself, and this negates the very foundation of spirituality. It is also believed that hatred harms more to the hating one than the hated one. The positive expression of a spiritual person is to love everyone without any reservation. It is again on the same belief that the Supreme One resides in every heart.

Hating someone also implies that you are better than the hated one. This is an expression of one's ego, which again is not justified on grounds of equality of all human beings and the fact that all beings originate from the same Supreme Power.

Jealousy arises because you cannot accept someone doing better than yourself. In a way this is also related to your egoistic thinking. In spiritual way of life, both hatred and jealousy are negative tendencies that need to be eradicated from your thinking mechanism. If you think all creation is the act of the Supreme Power, and that Supreme Power is impartial in its very being, then distinguishing one from another is to deny the just and fair nature of the Supreme. A spiritual person is supposed to be humble in behavior and must believe that all human beings are equal in the eyes of the Supreme Being. Hatred and jealousy therefore, are contradictory to the spiritual way of life.

Hatred and jealousy, in their extreme expression of negativity, lead to anger. All of these negative feelings arise from a bloated ego. Ego, in its negative expression, is partly inborn and partly attributed to wrong way of upbringing. It should be sublimated to its positive expression in healthy competition for self-good without causing any harm to others. Ego may enable one to rise in status and wealth but it does not make a person good in nature or spiritual in content.

Anger, in its extreme form, leads to violence. It is not only bad for the person to whom it is directed to, but also for the angry person also. It leads to physiological changes in the body that may take a while to return to normalcy. Frequent outbursts of anger make a person unhealthy in body and unpopular in behavior.

Much has been talked about anger management in books related to healthcare and social behavior. It is needless to say more since practically everyone has experienced the adverse effect of anger in his/her life. One way to manage it better is to follow the spiritual way. When the angry outburst comes, think of the Supreme One and pray. Keep reciting the name of the spiritual ideal, or idol if you worship one, till the anger subsides. When in argument with someone, if you find the argument leading to anger, better stop arguing than going further. Silence is golden in such situations. It also works in many opinion clashing situations.

Anger makes a person lose respect among colleagues, friends and even among strangers. It causes physical and mental stress that can be relieved by meditation. When it strikes, become silent, be still and meditate in whatever posture you are, sitting or standing. If you are facing an angry person, be sympathetic to his/her condition rather than return the anger by yourself becoming angry.

The habit of criticizing everybody and any event should be an avoidable trait. Some persons do it just for fun or just to spend time in idle gossip. Criticism is meant only for improving where it is required. It is not meant to amuse self or harming the reputation of others. Some people make criticism a profession, but that needs a high degree of responsibility and wisdom. One must see that it is meant to reform and not to degrade or hurt anyone badly. Back-biting is another form of criticism but only worse than that because it is always done in a negative manner.

A spiritual person always avoids idle gossip and hesitates to criticize adversely anyone since he is mentally trained to look for positivity in others and shower his love equally to all. To find fault in others is not his job. He always advises others to restrain from doing so. Offending others by any means is not in his blood. It is however true that some religious persons talk ill of others but it is a negative tendency and it is not advised if you are truly spiritual or truly religious. Amity and harmony are spiritual qualities and talking ill of others is unethical and unspiritual to say the least.

Intolerance and deceit are other two expressions of negativity in us. Intolerance of others' mistakes shows that one considers oneself above these faults. We forget that nobody is free from all faults. Everyone has some or the other deficiencies due to inborn incapacity to come to others' expectations. Spiritually speaking, tolerance is a quality that needs to be developed through proper training of mind. Study of social behavior and sticking to advices of social scientists can help. Availing the company of spiritual persons can also reduce this defect to some extent. Again, intolerance can lead to anger, which we have seen earlier is not good for us in any manner.

Deceiving others for personal gain is entirely out of spiritual domain. It amounts to sin in the language of religious practice. One may confuse this ability to deceive as an element of smartness but it is entirely wrong both from ethical and spiritual point of view. Craftiness is justified only for defeating evil and for no other reason. Deceiving innocent persons is nothing short of robbery. In the present competitive world, to take advantage of others by hook or crook for self gain is on the rise. But I see this as a sign of decline of ethical and moral standards rather than the rise of intellectual efforts. One must clearly understand the difference between deceit and intellectual smartness.

Fear is another deficiency in our emotional behavior. Among many types of fear, fear of death is most common and widespread. It is almost universally felt by everyone except those few, who are either brave soldiers or have become enlightened enough not to fear death. Fear of death implies loss of individuality in the living world, and all persons who have any ego dread this loss. It is also instinctual because nature wants to save the species. Saving one's life by all means is common to all species as an instinct. But man has the power to rationalize the life and its purpose and thereby get over the fear of death. In Hindu faith it is believed that one's soul does not die with the body and that it takes another body much as one change the clothes. Therefore, death is only a transitory change in the continuous cycle of birth and death. Fear of death in this context is thus meaningless.

We all have likes and dislikes. It starts from our very childhood. Something that pleases us we like it. Something that displeases us we dislike. This conditions our mind and we start favoring and disfavoring things and persons. If dislike rises to a higher level, it turns to hatred. If hatred increases, it turns to anger.

In spiritual parlance, it is advised for the seeker of spirituality to rise above the conditioning due to likes and dislikes. One is told to stay neutral to the impulses of likeness and dislike and remain calm under such emotional inputs. Such a training of mind keeps us away from the negative tendencies and consequent negative reactions, which otherwise put us under undesirable mental stresses and strains. In fact, the spiritual goal is to achieve unconditioned state of consciousness so as to be one with pure consciousness or the Super-consciousness.

Love is one of the strongest and most widely experienced positive emotions. It is felt by most of us during childhood as parental love and by parents as filial love. When we grow up we have friends loving friends and relatives. While married we experience it as love to or from the spouse. Even when we get old, we share the love of grandchildren. Of course, there are exceptions to this pattern of life, but I am saying this in general terms because most of us experience this in our worldly life.

Just like hatred has different shades of its expression, love too has many shades. These may be extreme likeness, simply attraction, obsession or extreme desire to possess. Love that is talked of in print and audiovisual media is not the love that I wish to elaborate. That kind of love is generally one person specific and is meant to entertain or bring tears to your eyes. What I want to refer to is the universal love. It is the love that we express equally to all beings. This is also the love that we experience from the Supreme Being. Universal love is for all creatures of the world and it is not one person specific. This is the spiritual form of love. It is pure and does not demand anything in return. Motherly love comes nearest to it but it is person specific, though parental love is generally same for all children.

The feeling of love is of supreme importance when we talk of the union of our consciousness with Supreme Consciousness. It is this emotion that helps us in devotional method for spiritual growth to divine level. Love of an ideal makes great heroes while love of the Supreme Being enables us to reach the state of salvation or the highest state of consciousness that is generally referred to as the enlightenment.

In spirituality, pure love for all beings in the universe is a sacred and soul lifting feeling. It is a credit to this feeling that some people place the power of love at the same footing as the power of the Supreme One. They perhaps say this because Supreme Being loves all its creation equally. In meditation we experience this feeling of love for all beings in the higher state of consciousness.

Love all is a great mantra for right living. It removes much of negativity within you. If you love all, there is no scope in your thinking to hate or feel jealous of anyone. It will purify your heart to a great extent. Love brings you near every living being while hatred takes you away. Love brings love in return; hatred brings anger and violence.

It is said that if you take one step of love towards the Supreme Being, the Supreme One takes two steps towards you. What better method could then be to spiritualize you? That is why, in the spiritual texts, the devotional method has been cited as the easiest method to reach the goal. Besides, this being the emotional way, everybody can practice it with ease without involving the intellectual interpretations of complex issues of philosophical nature. Anyway, intellect is not everybody's strong point while emotions are fairly widespread among humans.

A person desirous of following the path of ethics and spirituality must try to own the qualities of compassion and empathy. These qualities relate to a general feeling of concern to other person or persons in difficulty. One should not do this out of a sense of pity or superiority but as a duty of a person fortunate enough to help or serve others.

Helping others is always a noble gesture, worthy of a person of right living. Ideally, this gesture should be extended to all creatures and living beings of the world, since they all owe their origin to the same Supreme Power. This should be done with a sense of humility and service, rather than with the arrogance, or a condescending attitude, of a superior being or taking pity on an incompetent sufferer.

Concern for others should arise from the fact that we are all co-travelers on the road of existence on this planet and we all should share the resources of this earth with equal right. The great sages of the past knew it well and therefore, they prayed always for the welfare of all and not just for themselves.

One would expect that the seekers of spiritual goal, who went in isolation leaving the pleasures and comfort of the worldly life, would not care for the suffering masses. But this is a mistaken belief. Many sages of olden time greatly contributed to the society either by writing norms for right living or searching the ways to avoid suffering in life. They all wanted people to have a suffering-free life. In support of this view, I can state the shining example of Buddha who left the comforts and power of royal life and spent years in austerity and meditation to find a way for people to live without suffering. More recently, we all know about the contribution of swami Vivekananda and Sri Aurobindo who rekindled the spiritual awakening among the common people. No doubt there are many other examples in other faiths too when spiritually oriented persons gave their lives in the cause of ordinary people. I know of many saints in Christianity and gurus of Sikh faith who contributed greatly for the welfare of people but listing all of them would serve on greater purpose since I have already made the point.

Spiritual persons of most religions know the reality of existence and the common bond that unites all humanity. It is therefore, quite natural for them to feel concerned for others. It is part of spiritual training to understand this concern and make it integral to their way of life.

Forgiveness is a quality that is generally attributed to saintly people. Revenge and vengeance are common weaknesses of worldly people. But one must remember that forgiveness should be practiced from a position of strength, otherwise it has no meaning. Strength comes from strong body and well-trained mind. Spiritual people develop an inner strength through meditation and right living. Moreover, only people who commit mistakes and not crime deserve forgiveness. Habitual defaulters and incorrigible criminals deserve punishment as is the norm in most civilized societies. Judicial systems of most countries recognize this fact in the interest of people. Spiritual training helps in reducing the spirit of revenge and vengeance and promotes forgiveness for small mistakes. In general, it helps a lot if the spirit of revenge is replaced by the spirit of let go to avoid frequent mental stress.

Religious training of practically all faiths promotes charity as a necessary facet of life. It arises out of compassion and concern for people. Poverty has been a fact of life from times immemorial. The difference between haves and have-nots has remained with us for long as people have different capacities and capabilities for work and powerful people have refused to share the resources of nature with the less privileged ones. Charity therefore assumes importance from spiritual point of view as sharing comes from a sense of equality with others. Some people of spiritual orientation also insist that charity should be confined only to the deserving ones otherwise it will promote idleness in society.

There are two other points that are often talked of in connection with spiritual way of life. These are dispassion, and discrimination between right and wrong.

Dispassion essentially means avoidance of strong involvement with worldly things and events. The basic idea is to remain undisturbed in the pursuit of our goal by things that create extraneous thoughts and strong impressions in our mind and thereby take us away from the spiritual path. Some spiritual texts call it detachment from worldly attractions that are likely to take you away from spiritual practices such as meditation. It is said that only a dispassionate person is likely to be just, fair and impartial in judgment and objective and unbiased in opinion. In the present age of competitive and busy life, one is likely to take it to mean apathy towards the world. But one must understand the subtle difference in its interpretation. What it really implies is noninterference and avoiding meddlesome behavior in things and events that could obstruct our path of right living. Strong involvement leaves strong impressions in our mind. For a spiritual person, an observer's way of life is a better option than getting deeply involved in the unspiritual affairs of the world. In case you are not clear about the observer's way of life, let me illustrate it by citing first two lines of a song by the great singer KL Sehgal, who sang it some eighty years ago. The lines, when translated in English read as follows: 'I am in the world but I am not desirous of it; I have passed through the market but I am not a buyer. Essentially it stresses the point that you need not be carried away by the glitter of the attractions of this world. '

Literally dispassion would mean acting without being passionate about everything. In spiritual terms, dispassion has been talked about a lot in the sense of an observer's way of life. You do duties but without getting too much actively involved in affairs that distract your mind from the spiritual goal. Some may say that this tendency of avoiding strong involvement in the affairs of the world may be counterproductive in our getting success in this competitive world. But you must remember that success in worldly affairs is not necessarily success in spiritual growth. The spiritual quality helps us to lead the right kind of life, life without worries and emotional stress.

The quality of discrimination implies the ability to distinguish between right and wrong, real and unreal and so on. In spiritual terms, the only thing that is real is the Supreme Power. This is because it is the only thing that is eternal and unchanging. All other things being short lived are unreal. The right path of living is the ethical and spiritual path. Discrimination therefore, has to be applied in this context.

The ability to discriminate in this sense is quite rare since most people consider the material world as real whereas the reality is otherwise. We have stated earlier that the Supreme Reality is the Pure Consciousness and not the material world as we see it. Those who can discriminate between right and wrong way of life and the real and unreal material existence are indeed very few in this world. But this quality can be cultivated through spiritual knowledge and spiritual practice. That is why spiritually enlightened persons insist that people should understand what is right and what is real.

The last point, but not the least important, is the need to surrender to the Supreme Power. This surrender comes naturally to that person who knows the infinite extent, the eternal existence and the vast power of the Supreme Being. All our prayers, meditation and worship should be done with the spirit of surrender to the Supreme. This surrender reduces ego and hence the feeling of individuality. It is like a river losing itself in the sea. On complete surrender, the Supreme One takes over your thoughts and will. Once our will merges with that of the Supreme One, we rise from human to the divine.

The seekers of spiritual path are always advised not to forget the power of the Supreme ever. That is the only truth of this universe. That is ever existing and never changing. The existence of everything, living or nonliving, depends on that.

***

Be Positive

Standing in a garden of flowers do not talk of thorns. Be positive if you want to enjoy life.

Do not curse the world for your loneliness. Nobody is ever alone. The Supreme one is always with everyone at all times. The trouble is not all consider the Supreme one as their friend. Trust in that power and you will never feel alone.

What is the Shape of the Supreme Being?

If I were to reply the question 'what is the shape of the Supreme One?' I would say the following:

The Supreme One has no shape but it is present in all shapes. Just as any fluid takes the shape of the vessel or container in which it is poured; similarly, the Supreme one takes the shape as per the imagination of the viewer. After all, the ultimate reality is an invisible entity that exists throughout the cosmos and is the cause of everything in the universe. It is pure consciousness that has existence but no fixed name or shape. Enlightened persons see it differently but agree on its infinite power and eternal existence.

Do not waste time and energy in wanting to look for evidence of the existence of the Supreme One. Instead, try to feel its presence anywhere or everywhere and you will be amply rewarded.

Intention Matters

Sin and virtue, ethical and unethical, good and bad work depends on our intention in working. If we donate with the intention of getting name and fame then it is not a virtue. Similarly, when some persons and organizations make big charitable promises to people in order to improve their image and then intentionally forget to comply later when their purpose is served, they commit sin and not virtue. It is a great sin to give false hopes to anyone.

No doubt sin and virtue are relative terms and there is nothing absolute about it. There is always some good and some bad in all our works sometime our good intention can also harm others. But the point I make is always keep your intention good and clean. That is all that matters when we work.

9
Contacts with Nature

Remaining in contact with nature is a part of right living. As with trees and plants so also with us, we get our nourishment from our roots, be it our parents or ancestors or the mother earth. Nature provides us food in the form of grains and fruits through crops and trees, while the carnivorous eat the s animals which again depend on nature for their food.

Nature sustains myriad of species with its vast resources. All our things of comfort also come from nature in one form or another. In addition, it provides great sights and plentiful water for all living beings that is so vital for their existence.

Nature not only provides for our body; it gladdens our heart with fine emotions to sooth our mind. Even a painting of a flower makes us happy. Think of how much pleasure you get by smelling a live flower. The scenic beauty that nature bestows on us is so fascinating that only a stone- hearted person will ever ignore it.

The nature of man is such that instead of feeling grateful to our sustainer and savior, we destroy and pollute it much too often. We cut the tress, pollute the air, spoil the rivers and kill the animals for food or fun. When nature reacts through floods, storms and untimely weather variations in season, we blame not ourselves but nature for it. This is ingratitude of high order.

The sight of a garden of flowers and colorful plants is a soul lifting experience. It lifts our mood and refreshes our mind. We are really unfortunate if we miss such sights and experiences and remain glued to our technological toys and gadgets instead.

The wise men of Vedic age divided the human life into four parts of twenty-five years each. The first was for education and learning, the second for producing wealth, raising a family and fulfilling desires, the third for spiritual studies and meditation while the fourth was for renunciation and introspection. The whole idea was to live the normal life as well as work for salvation. In this way of life, most of the time was spent in the lap of nature; the first part was spent in guru's school, away from city life while third and fourth parts were also spent away from the worldly ways of city life. One may of course, argue that those days were very different from the present ones and that there was no pressure of technical jobs that demand one's living in cities for learning and practicing the skills of today. The circumstances are different now and hence the old practices are difficult to follow in the present age of technology and competition. I agree the times have changed now, but at the same time the need to live with nature still stands. Our body structure, feelings and emotions still feel the need for fresh air, clean water and nourishing elements that nature only can provide. From time to time, we have to release our stress of living in overcrowded and polluted environment by renewing our contact with nature. Going to gardens and parks, long drives to wooded forests, climbing hills, rowing on the lakes and rivers and appreciating the beauty of nature are desirable activities that add to the quality of life and refresh our body and mind. In this sense these are important necessary for living the right kind of life

Enjoyment in open spaces is far superior to playing in claustrophobic small rooms. But some people whose lives are conditioned for living indoor all the time still prefer to visit malls than go to a city park.

Children need to play in parks and playgrounds and engage in sports that are good for their physical and mental health. Instead, unfortunately, they are spending time in video games in confined rooms that do no good to their physical development. The shortage of space in city life may be a handicap, but if people pressurize the administration in the interest of their children, to keep suitable and sufficient space for their children's plying fields it would help in the proper growth of the future generation. It is a sad spectacle to see children playing on roads and risking their lives. In crowded colonies they get the wrath of residents if they play near the houses and break the window glasses.

Tourism to places of nature's beauty, especially to hill resorts, hiking and long walks in forests, also helps to satisfy the natural urge to be in contact with nature. Those who can afford do so by finding sufficient time and money are indeed fortunate. They come back happy and refreshed to carry out further work with greater efficiency. But not everyone is capable enough to find resources for such relaxation.

Most people in the common bracket take to religious tourism visiting places of religious significance. This serves double purpose of coming in contact with nature as well as satisfying their religious sentiments. Fortunately, most of the temples in the country are situated in remote place rich with greenery; at hill tops or in caves or at places which requires physical and mental effort to reach the destination. Possibly, this was purposely done to test the determination, sincerity and high emotional attachment of the religious tourist for the sacred place. Many people go there to fulfill their vows and wishes for a better life and to tide over their difficulties and sufferings. Religious tourism all over the world is quite large. This is profitable for business too. Indeed, it is of great benefit to the individual as well as to the economic activity of the place.

Interest in gardening and plant life also satisfies the desire to be with nature. I have personally felt a great mental relief from tiresome work when I worked in my garden. Seeing the seeds taking roots and coming up as plants is a happy experience. To find your effort blooming into flowers, and then fruits, gives enormous pleasure. To eat what you have grown gives you a better taste than otherwise, even though this difference is only a psychological one. Even those who live in crowded colonies in big cities can experience this pleasure by having potted plants on terraces or balconies. If you have the inclination, you can certainly find a way to bring a piece of nature in your life.

When you see a flower or a waterfall, you are transported to a different world; a world that is free of the worries of meeting deadlines and competing ventures. There are many small pleasures that you can derive from nature. For example, experience the feeling when standing on a beach the sea waves come and wet your feet. Similarly, watch the bird make its nest, look at the photograph of earth taken by a satellite and wonder its magnificent blue color, stand in open with the cool moonlight shining on you in summer evening or warm sunlight making you comfortable in cold winter and so on. I find a tree laden with fruit a very pleasant and worthy sight to watch and then be happy at nature's benevolence.

If you love the Supreme One, love its creation too. You will see the Supreme in every small thing, living or nonliving, in its vast creation and wonder at its hidden presence. You will start loving the Supreme if you calmly watch the night sky and gratefully acknowledge the starry kingdom of nature. When you see the wide variety of plants, fishes, animals, birds and humans, your heart will at once melt in reverence and awe towards the Supreme One. You cannot but surrender to its power to create such variety, such beauty and sheer brilliance of the created objects. Nature takes you to such spiritual thoughts provided you care for nature.

Appreciation of nature, and the desire to be with it, is certainly a noble quality that must be nurtured by all. It is, and should be, a part of right living.

***

Count Your Blessings

Count your blessings and not miseries. It gives you reason to be grateful to nature, the great giver. You have eyes which many people are denied. You have the speech and hearing which many people do not have. If you have a full body and good health, you are indeed fortunate compared to those who are not so lucky. In addition, if you are capable to earn two meals a day you should be thankful for that. If you have strength enough to help somebody, you should feel fortunate to be so compared to the weak and old.

Always feel blessed and not unfortunate because the great giver has given you enough to lead a comfortable life. Do not doubt the giver's kindness, sense of justice and benevolence. Do not blame anybody for your miseries. They could be due to your own wrong judgment, mistaken beliefs or simply circumstantial compulsions. Believe in yourself and your ability to pass over temporary difficulties.

Let our Upbringing Include Ethics and Spirituality

Generally, in most cases, for various reasons, we think and act imperfectly. Partly it is due to lack of spiritual content in our thought and consequently in our actions. We ignore the role of spiritual training in our bringing up. This is done even by those who are well read and competent professionals. We think spirituality is for the old and idle persons who have dissociated themselves from the mainstream of life. Unfortunately, this is a mistaken belief and a retrograde step in the development of human personality. The role of spirituality in our life is highly underrated by the present society. It is partly due to over emphasis of technology in our everyday life.

Live A Useful Life

If you think life is meaningless, find a purpose to live. It could be learning a skill that you do not possess, serve and care someone you love and respect, help the weak and the needy, or simply share with others what you have. It will give a meaning to your life. If you find life dull and monotonous, give your time to explore nature. It has mystery, excitement and a variety of activities that will engage you usefully for a long time. If you find the world uncaring, there is enough in the plant and animal life that needs you. It will give enough reward in return in the form of love and loyalty.

People want eternal existence in a world where nothing lives forever. They should instead be making full use of what time they have. If you are too critical of the opinion of others, learn to accept the differences and the variety in nature.

The invisible need not be nonexistent. It is just that we do not possess the eyes to see it.

10
Three Types of Natural Qualities

A person is judged by the qualities he/she displays in reaction to his/her interaction with others. Some of the qualities are picked up in upbringing, the company one keeps, or simply advised by wise persons. The parents, teachers and friends thus play a role in the outward nature of a person. But spiritually speaking, there are some inherent or inborn qualities that decide the nature of a person. Bhagwadgita has described three types of such qualities that characterize people according to their natural tendencies. These are,1 goodness oriented, 2 action oriented and 3 lazy and ignorant. Since these tendencies are inborn, we call them natural qualities.

The first type, the good-natured ones, display virtue, righteousness, piousness, honesty and truthfulness. The person has a balanced mind, a serene and harmonious nature and is focused on living in the present and desires self- improvement. These are the traits suited for spiritual development and hence desirable. Such a person is characterized by happiness, contentment, patience, perseverance, forgiveness and spiritual yearning. These traits arise from purity of head and heart, positive attitude towards life and a virtuous bent of mind. The whole purpose of including spirituality in one's thinking is to inculcate such qualities so as to rise to a higher state of consciousness.

The second, the action-oriented type, is active, dynamic, and desirous of achievement, authority and power. He works for personal gain and believes in doing work with passion and consistency. He is aggressive by temperament and believes in building great plans for future. He is impulsive in behavior and prone to violence. He is competitive and materialistic in worldly affairs.

The third type, lazy and ignorant, are dull and low activity people. They have no desire to understand the higher knowledge and lack wisdom. They are lethargic and regressive in approach to life. They live in the past and have no vision for higher aims of life. They stand for darkness, illusion, quiescence, passivity and pessimism. They like rest, and inertia. They are prone to greed, and criminal offences. Their minds are generally in doubt, and not clear about any issue. They have great attachment to worldly matters and do not hesitate even to harm others.

The three types have a different likeness for food as well. The first type likes simple food, preferably fruits and milk and does not care for tasty but unhealthy food. The second type likes delicious, tasty and heavy food including the non-vegetarian dishes. The third type does not mind eating stale, overcooked or undercooked food.

Generally, every person has all the three qualities in some proportion. These become apparent when appropriate circumstances arise. For example, given the circumstances, a good-natured person may become angry and lose his cool against provocation of extreme nature. Similarly, an action-oriented person may help a weak person if the occasion so demands. Also, if the lazy person is given sufficient encouragement by way of reward or profitable proposition, he may agree to serve the benefactor against his slothful nature. In many cases however, one quality may dominate over other two and thereby determine the person's nature. Sometimes more than one quality may dominate. In any case, the effort should be made to rise towards the goodness quality that is helpful for right living.

For those who believe in the Karma theory, the natural qualities may hold special significance. Karma theory, in brief, states that the present conditions of living, pleasure or suffering depend on the result of past actions. It applies to the cycle of birth and death, meaning thereby that your present tendencies might be the result of your actions in the past life, much as your present situation at the moment might be the result of your past actions in this life as well. Some people may take Karma theory as a pessimistic one since you become helpless in your present condition because of your bad Karma in the past. But I believe this is not the right way to look at it. Your present life, even with bad destiny, gives you a chance to improve your Karma in this life because of the free will granted to you. This, I think, is the purpose of life. Take the chance of this life and do good deeds to improve your level of consciousness. This can be done through living a life of ethics and spirituality, which will eventually raise your consciousness to higher levels.

For right living, ethical and spiritual component of our mind body structure is important. For this, we must try to discipline our mind and body to adopt the qualities that are desirable for building our character and conduct of high order so that we aim for a higher state of consciousness. This is the purpose of spiritually oriented life. Such a life is good for self as well as for others. This is what I call the balanced way of life.

***

Desire for Happiness

We search for happiness in every moment. This could be a fruitless attempt for many people but this is desirable or even necessary for living. This gives us hope that takes us forward. Without this life would be dull and monotonous. Knowing full well that getting happiness every moment is impossible, we still run around all our life for it. Some people understand this and adopt a detached approach which brings stillness in life. Some people call this approach to stillness as wisdom. Most people get this wisdom in the later part of life when perhaps it is too late.

11
Performances of Duties

Every person has some rights and duties when living in a society. These are sanctioned by the social and governmental authorities and expected to be followed by every individual member of the group that forms a nation. In a multi religious and multiracial country they may vary a little on grounds of religious sanctions but the ideal thing is to follow the same rules and regulations by all the citizens equally. Practically every religion has codified its way of life and put these in their religious books. However, on humanistic ground, some duties are binding on people to adhere irrespective of their religious or social affiliations.

In general, we are more concerned with our rights than our duties. Apart from this being a human weakness, it is also because our instinct of survival and self-interest overpowers our thinking mechanism. This is against the principle of right living. It is necessary therefore, to train our mind with self-discipline and spiritual advice to counter such self-seeking interests. This will give right place to duties in our life.

Performance of duties is part of right living. We have obligations to those who make our life worth living. We owe gratitude to our parents, teachers, elders, professional employers, to nature, society and the country.

Our parents give life to us, and thereby a chance to improve our actions in this life, so that we may raise our consciousness, from spiritual point of view, to higher levels. They provide us an intelligence that is denied to other species. They give us love and care and protect us from dangers and difficulties. They rear us up like a tender plant in a wild forest.

The teachers give us education, which enables us to pick up skills that can give us the ability to earn our livelihood. They also broaden our vision in many other fields that helps us to be a responsible citizen. Spiritual teachers show us the path to another world that lies within us and is the source of power to our mind and body.

Elders give us the benefit of their experience of life, which helps us tackle many problems. They tell us how we should deal with others in order to safe guard our interest in this selfish world. They protect us and warn us against future problematic situations that may threaten our peace and prosperity if we are not careful enough. They truly love us and have our welfare at heart. They also advise us and stand with us whenever we need their help.

Our professional employers may not be as much interested in our private life as the elders and relatives, but they provide us the means of livelihood which is an essential requirement for living with honor. This is no less favor and we should be grateful for that. Of course, we also work hard for this chance to serve but still they deserve respect and sincerity from us as their due.

I have already talked about our connection with nature and the gratitude we owe to it. Nature is an important factor in providing resources for the buildup of our mind and body.

We are bound with society in a number of ways. We share the security, the customs, the festivals and many other activities that give us pleasure and enjoyment in our social circle. Often, they are a great help in our difficulties too. Our gratitude to our country goes without saying as it provides security to us from lawless elements, foreign enemies and from those who are out to grab our fundamental rights of freedom, liberty and equality.

To each of the above benefactors, it is incumbent on us to do our duty to them. That is what we call paying our debt to them for their love to us. Foremost among all of them are our parents. We need to obey them in childhood and take care of them in their old age. But some in the young age generation today think otherwise. They think it was parent's duty to bring us up and prepare us to face the world as other animals and birds do it in nature. One may go as far as saying that it is the right of children to get love and care from their parents. But they must remember that along with rights come duties too. If it is our right to get love and care from the parents, it is our duty to give it back when they need it. The Hindu scripture have stated very clearly that we owe a debt to our parents and teachers because they give us a body and make us knowledgeable, capable and worth contributing to society. Mother has also been given the status of the first teacher. Those who fail to comply with their duty towards parents they are committing a blunder that is unforgiveable by the laws of society. Of course, as some youngsters of present age may point out, parents at times can be irrational and dominating and refuse to give freedom of choice to their children. But this does not absolve them from the debt, and In spite of opinion clash, the duty of children towards parents does not vanish. Even while living away from parents, they need to keep track of their difficulties and provide help as best as they can. In the modern age of technology and logic, the emotional attachment is losing ground as is often seen when children settle abroad for their personal benefit and lose sight of their parents back home.

The helpless parents are left to fend for themselves and they lead a lonely life with an emotional vacuum in their hearts.

The respect for teachers in this age is diminishing. The strong bond that existed between the teacher and the taught earlier is no longer seen in today's class rooms. It has become merely a business venture where the teacher gets paid for his/her work and the students pay for that. I am reminded of a time in my childhood when the teacher took pride in the progress of the student and even went so far as to take extra classes free for those who were weak in studies. May be the present environment is no longer conducive for such benevolence. But at least a bond of concern and care between the student and teacher is needed in the interest of both. Unless this bond is there, knowledge and wisdom of the teacher will not pass smoothly to the student. It stands to reason that there must be respect for the giver of knowledge from the receiver of that knowledge.

Spiritual gurus, or more specifically spiritual masters, have always had a place of respect and reverence in most religious societies. I am not talking of the class of priesthood which every religion has, nor of the self-styled gurus or babas that assume spiritual authority for their own welfare. I am talking of genuine spiritually enlightened persons who have attained spiritual powers by dint of rigorous spiritual practices and meditation over long periods and then out of concern for common people they advise them to adopt ethical and spiritual way of life. Their love for uplift of society is genuine and they consider their social responsibility a work for the Supreme. No doubt such persons deserve our deepest regards and respect and we must help their cause for our own good. They generally spread love and brotherhood for the general welfare of all. We must consider it our duty to follow their advice and join their effort of spreading spiritual way of life. This will help in maintaining peace and harmony in society and will promote right living.

We cannot expect the value system of gurukul tradition these days but at least the teaching these days can contain some elements of ethics, morality and spirituality to prepare the child for right living. This will not only benefit the teacher student relationship but also will improve the general environment of society where values and respect for law will prevail. I believe rationality and respect for old values can coexist and they are good for any right-thinking society. You may not believe in the religious myths but maintaining ethical principles will only do well for everyone.

Duty to elders lies in paying them respect that is due to them. They shower so much love to the young ones. The young ones can at least be courteous and respectful to them.

To professional employers, you can be sincere in work and look after the interest of the organization as part of your duty. Of course, the relationship is strictly like business. You work and they pay. There is no scope for emotions. And yet, truthfulness and sincerity are required in this two-way association. The employers too need to look after the interest of the employees because their welfare is also indirectly helpful to the organization. An atmosphere of distrust and servant master attitude can vitiate the environment for work.

Our main duty to nature lies in living in harmony with it and not as an exploiter of it. Nature in general is quite generous in giving its resources equally to all but there should be a limit to the greed of man in using these. Putting untreated sewage in the rivers is a crime of great magnitude. Technology should not only be used for our comfort but for protecting the nature too.

This should be done at individual level as well as at the organizational level since both are beneficiary of nature.

Our duty to society lies in living ethically and accepting and acting according to rule of law. Law breaking is an offence punishable gy law enforcing agencies. But self-discipline will go a long way in reducing the workload of police and judiciary. Right living is a step in this direction.

Duty towards the country is not only the job of professional soldiers but also the duty of every citizen. Harming the country by illegal activities is injurious to the interests of the country. It hurts the economy and peaceful environment of the country and innocent people suffer the most from such harmful activities.

All in all, whereas we get our rights from nature, society and the laws of the land, we also inherit some obligations and duties that we have to perform as a good citizen. Living according to the law of land and the law of nature is part of right living. It is good for us as individuals as well as for the society or the community to which we belong.

***

The Religion of A Spiritually Enlightened Person

The mental level of spiritually advanced persons is such that all religions lose their significance as separate identity. For them, all humanity is one and there is only one objective, that of making a contact with the source of all creation. Supreme power for them holds true for all religions. You will not find any true spiritually enlightened person distinguishing one religion from another. For them all religions meet at one point, the creator of all. Different names and forms are just the creation of one Supreme Power that resides in all. Therefore, it is futile to ask a spiritually high person what religion he/she belongs to.

We Live in A World of Duality

We live in a world of duality and life is a game of truth and falsehood, sin and virtue, pleasure and suffering, cruelty and mercy, belief and doubt, love and hatred, peace and conflict, work and leisure, liberty and bondage, wealth and poverty, justice and injustice, birth and death, knowledge and ignorance, goodness and evil, greed and generosity. In playing this game of life, we get so busy that we forget our true identity

Our life is like passing through a jungle with no clear path for moving forward. But we are given two vehicles. One moves very fast but it is likely to crash any time. It is named evil. The other vehicle moves slowly but it has provision for deciding what is the right path and what is not. It is named goodness. The driver is the ego and intellect is the navigator. Our free will is the decider to choose the vehicle. Whether we reach the destination and in what condition depends on our choice of vehicle and the way we drive. Nobody is to be blamed for what happens to us.

12
Thoughts and Actions

Our thoughts and actions make our living right or wrong. Every activity starts from a thought. Therefore, if we want to live right, we must think right.

Our thoughts originate from our conditioning of mind, the events and ideas stored in our subconscious, our present circumstances in which we live and our natural tendencies we inherit. The whole thought process is a complex affair. Our growth and build-up of personality is a direct outcome of our thought process.

It is not only the origin of thoughts, but also the processing of information and interpretation of sense signals, influence our behavior and actions. There is a complex neuron circuitry that comes into play. Our intellect, our emotions, even our psychology, all affects our actions.

Spirituality lays great stress on the training of mind that affects both our body and mind. For example, meditation directly affects both in a positive manner. On the contrary, if we focus on wrong ideas and events, we can slide down to disastrous consequences. The study and practice of spirituality under right environment is an important factor for correcting our way of life and for the healthy growth of body and mind.

What goes into our subconscious? The words, the sights and events that leave a strong impression on us finally settle down in our subconscious. the related thoughts come up from time to time and constitute our involuntary thoughts. If these are unworthy of actions, they need to be rejected by the spiritually trained mind to avoid wrong actions. This needs a strong will. Those who succumb to these wrong actions face the miserable consequences. Strong will and proper judgment are thus very important for staying on the right path.

It is advised in spiritual circles that you should stay away from involving strongly in temptations and attractions of the world that lead you astray in life. The reason is that strong impressions will accumulate in your subconscious and will resurface when they are not required.

The best way to avoid the effect of wrong thoughts is to ignore them rather than suppress them. Suppression strengthens such thoughts while ignoring them will make them die a natural death. Practicing frequently to ignore them will ultimately strengthen your will to live without them. Such thoughts will then lose their strength to influence you.

Conditioning of mind starts from early childhood when the child comes into contact with environment. Every interaction leaves an impression on the mind. Some of the most effective impressions the child gets from parents. That is why parents have a great role to play in the mental growth of the child. In Hindu households, we call the parental conditioning as Samskaras (psychological inputs) which play an important part later in adult life. The child gets the ideas of good and bad from parents first and later from others.

Conditioning has much to do with spiritual aspect of our personality. A spiritual philosopher pointed out that to experience the Super consciousness one must unlearn what he/she has learnt from books, even the spiritual books. What he really emphasized was that our mind conditioned by worldly knowledge was not able to experience the state of no-thought. To experience Super consciousness, one must be in the intervening space between two thoughts. In short, one must be in the thoughtless state. This is possible only when our mind is capable of dispelling all thoughts, good or bad. It is our thoughts that arise from our conditioned mind that prove an obstacle to self-realization or to reach the state of absolute reality.

The fundamental reason of conditioning is our natural reaction of pleasure and displeasure. Our preferences and prejudices constitute the conditioned state. Something that pleases us we like something that displeases us we dislike. That is why in spiritual training it is advised that we must rise above our likes and dislike because these create strong impressions that stay in our memory of the conscious mind and then finally permeate to subconscious. Spiritual advice has always emphasized that we musts rise above these tendencies, and consider every sense input dispassionately.

Our conditioning by interaction with worldly people and things does not stop at any particular age. It is a continuous process that goes on all our life. The earlier we understand the role of conditioning in our life the better it will be. It will enable us to correct our worldly behavior in time to avoid wrong impressions. These wrong impressions change our very nature and thereby put us in difficult situations. It is wise to choose our associates and friends with fair degree of proper judgment and careful thought. Even if we are confident that we cannot be influenced by bad company, and the wrong ways of others, we must remember that every interaction has its effect on us, directly or indirectly. The wrong impressions can enter our subconscious without our being conscious of it. We must always apply our ability to discriminate between right and wrong in every thought and action. Impulsive actions can put us to regrettable situations more often than we think. In matters of ethics and spirituality, it is all the more significant since they affect our right way of living. Proper sense of discrimination and right judgment are necessary qualities for a right living person.

De-conditioning is a very difficult process and very few people can succeed in this effort. Long hours of introspection and meditation are required for this. But as they say, prevention is better than cure, it is important to be careful about creating deep impressions that are made by passionate involvement in our dealings with worldly affairs.

13
Listening to Conscience

We are all gifted by nature to have conscience that takes us correctly through the maze of right and wrong actions in this world. It is part of our mental faculty. It gives us a feeling of unease, when we either do something wrong ourselves or see other persons doing so. Religious- minded people have termed conscience as the inner voice or the voice of the Supreme one, though psychologists would differ with this view. Whatever picture we may paint of it, it is an ability we all share in some measure to know right from wrong with advantage, provided we care to listen to it.

Those who are fortunate to have a highly developed conscience are better placed to lead an ethical and spiritual life than those who have a very feeble inner voice to guide them. Conscience can be developed through believing and honoring the ethical values of life. The more you care for these values in your actions, the stronger the conscience becomes. On the other hand, those who repeatedly ignore the voice of conscience, they weaken this voice. We weaken our conscience when we act with a bloated ego, an arrogant intellect or condition our mind by preferences and prejudices.

When we purify our mind by sticking to ethics and spirituality, we nourish our ability to distinguish between right and wrong.

By repeatedly doing so, we strengthen our conscience. It helps in balancing the mind. With a balanced mind we can walk on the right path in life.

Our observations of actions around us affect our thinking. In our childhood if we see our parents breaking the rules of society we also tend to do so. Our respect for our parents makes us think that what they do is the right thing to do. This distorts our value system and our conscience is silenced. But if our parents tell us what is right and what is wrong, as per the social laws and human values, our judgment about right and wrong will be corrected and our conscience will get a boost. In more ways than one, our friends, colleagues, elders, relatives and close associates all affect our sense of right and wrong one way or the other.

We are all members of a society which we want to be livable and good for all. It is necessary therefore, that each member of the society appreciates this fact and lives according to socially acceptable rules of conduct and knows what is good and what is not so good. But judgment of conscience is not only about social laws framed by humans but also about universal human values as well. As I said before, universal human values have a touch of divine. Nobody in the world would say that truth, purity, love and concern for others are not right. These values are built into our system by nature for right living. But our free will takes us away from these values for selfish reasons.

Even if society has erred in framing laws against human values for collective selfish reasons, such as annexing others land by force and violence, the conscience will revolt against this since the conscience is related to universal human values that guarantees freedom for all. In this sense, conscience works at a higher level than merely acting on the acceptance of socially acceptable rules of conduct as right or wrong. Conscience gives us the judgment of the Supreme One, or the nature if you like, while the social laws reflect the opinion of the majority of the people in society who frame the laws. In this sense, I consider conscience as divine

We tend to act in our personal interest while society does so in the collective sense. Our conscience follows what is right in universal sense. Divinity and nature have universal appeal. Therefore, listening to conscience is like following the way of the universal creator, which is the way of right living. Spiritual commandments are also correct in the universal sense irrespective of any regional or local relevance.

Conscience gives a moral sense of right and wrong. In that sense it is different from intuition. Some people intuitively know whether something or some activity is right or wrong. But they do not know why it is so. Conscience works at the conscious level while intuition works at the level of intuitive thinking. Both may be divine in a sense since the source is the same Supreme Power. Only the levels of working are different.

Conscience is a positive emotion. Every day we come across situations where it is required to be exercised but we ignore it in our self-interest, either under pressure of ego or under arrogance of intellect. For right living it is imperative that we develop it through ethical and spiritual practices and make a habit of listening to it before we act. For acting on the voice of conscience, we need to have courage of conviction. Development of strong conscience is certainly a plus point in the psychological growth of human personality. For a morally right person, the inner sensitivity comes from inner purity and clarity of mind. Empathy and virtue enhance it. Our conscience is a measure of our moral strength, which is an important and necessary aspect of right living.

***

Inner Light

Human being is a psychophysical structure that contains the physical body (gross), mind (subtle), and according to some religious and philosophical traditions, a third part called soul. Soul is the spiritual part that is believed to continue after the death of body. It is the subtlest part, and being spiritual is akin to spirit. But some religious beliefs do not connect it to spirit, even though the word spiritual is a derivative of the word spirit. This immaterial part is believed to reside in every person near about the position of heart and separates from the body at death. Soul is believed to be eternal, and according to Bhagwadgita, it changes the body at rebirth. Thus, it is soul that goes on changing bodies in the birth and death cycle of life. In all these cycles it remains unchanging and ever living.

Soul also has been defined as an essence or actuating cause of an individual life. But according to Hindu religious belief, soul in individual is a part of the cosmic reality, the Super-consciousness. In this sense, it is the very reality of a person, the life principle that is behind the functioning of the body and mind.

Soul in its abstract form is the knowledge and bliss. It is eternal, unchanging and connected with the Divine. The religious philosophers call it the Truth of existence of everything in the universe. In human body, it is confined but in its universal existence, it is infinite, eternal, all-powerful, all-knowing, all-seeing, and present everywhere. In its creative principle, it is the cause of everything, living or nonliving.

The soul embedded in our body is knowledge and bliss in its abstract form. But when it is given a form understandable by everyone, it is called inner light because knowledge is synonymous with light while darkness signifies ignorance. The Vedas also state that the soul, whether it lies within us or in its universal context, is self-luminous. This literally means that it is all knowledge itself. It does not require any light (knowledge) from anywhere else. The spiritually advanced persons come in contact with the experience of seeing the light (knowledge) when they go inward and meditate on the Super-consciousness. They see the ultimate reality of our existence in its true form.

14
Need for Introspection

We are habituated to seek everything and every answer to our problem from the outside working world. We never acknowledge that within us there is power to find solutions to our physical and mental problems. For that however, we need to turn inward from time to time and introspect. It is necessary to know how we can apply midcourse correction to our psychological and spiritual behavior towards outside world and at the same time keep harmony in our body mind structure. In addition, there are some philosophical questions such as what is our true reality, what keeps us disturbed in spite of our best efforts, where do we go wrong in our actions even with best of intentions and so on.

Wise persons of the past and spiritual personalities of every age have repeatedly told us that many answers can best be found through going inward and seeking the solution from introspection and meditating on the Supreme Being. As I said earlier, the Supreme is knowledge and bliss. It can provide us both knowledge and keep us in peace provided we pursue our quest with sincere efforts at spiritualizing ourselves.

The inward world is as complex as the world outside. It can provide answers to our problems and questions intuitively. One of the most difficult questions is what our true reality is and what the purpose of our existence is. Again, what sort of relationship we need to adopt with nature. There are some other questions of mundane nature like whether our thoughts and actions are relevant to our existence as a human being, why are we so self-centered and why don't we act globally in the interest of all.

Our spiritual reality is within us. To seek it we have to turn inward. For this, we have to turn our senses from outward to inward. This cuts off most of the irrelevant inputs from our senses and calms our mind. If we close our eyes, almost eighty percent of the total input to our brain is cut off. By closing years, another ten to twelve percent is removed. It then makes our mind free to focus on issues of our deeper concern. We can then analyze our thoughts and consequent actions and decide where did we go wrong and where we altered from the path of right living. This kind of exercise is at least required from time to time to keep us on the right path.

We are deeply influenced by our tendencies and emotions. Do we then think there is a need to apply brakes to our passionate and fast going life? We are conditioned to work in our slf interest and deeply involve matters that are irrelevant to our higher goals of life. We need to balance our thoughts and actions to keep all the three parts of our life, namely body, mind and spiritual. we need to nourish our body with balanced food, purify our mind by removing thoughts that that create negativity in our conscious and subconscious mind, and devote sufficient time for spiritualizing our inner life.

In simple terms introspection has been defined as the process of thinking deeply and carefully to examine our own ideas, feelings etc. It relies on observations of one's mental state. It basically deals with psychology but spirituality also has its advantages in being self-aware. We practice meditation to better understand our inner self.

In introspection there are some points worth keeping in view. The first is that you must ask yourself what questions and not why questions. For example, you must ask what makes you sad instead of why I am sad. Secondly, you must be more mindful. Thirdly, you must expand your curiosity and lastly you must spend more time alone, doing nothing but thinking deeply and reflecting on thoughts, emotions and memories and examine what they mean.

There are some benefits of introspection but there are some demerits also. Therefore, you have to practice it under the watchful eyes of a teacher, whether a psychologist or a spiritual teacher. It can be helpful in mental health treatment involving psychotherapy or in advancing in spiritual domain by meditation. It can also be a great source of personal knowledge. It can provide knowledge that is not possible in any other way. It can help make connections between different experiences and their responses. More importantly it can improve capacity for empathy and can help you make better decisions.

Unguided and careless practice of introspection can lead to rumination that is going over thoughts again and again.

The object of my including introspection in this book is to point out the need to think inwardly as a part of spiritual effort. For the more seriously minded seekers it can have a greater role in their spiritual practices such as meditation but for a common person who is only interested in leading right kind of life, it may be a time-to-time reflection of a few minutes, done frequently to put the thoughts and actions in proper perspective. The objective is to stay on the right path of balanced life in which all the three parts, body, mind and spirituality are properly balanced to keep life happy and useful.

***

Worship the Supreme Being out of Love and Not for Fear or Favour

Most of us actions are for benefit of our self. This is guided by both instinct of survival as well as because of our conditioned thinking. Our religious sentiment is also not free of such considerations. In prayer and worship, most of us ask for this and that from the Supreme One that will either relieve us from pain and malady or provide us a prosperous life that will make our living comfortable. In short, we are deeply concerned with our requirement of health and wealth. Some however, go as far as causing harm to their enemies and pray to the Supreme One for help in such nefarious activities.

In the self-driven world of today, very few devotees of the Supreme pray and worship out of love for the Supreme. The truth however is that only the loving devotees are qualified to be called the real admirers of the Supreme. Only their worship has any real meaning.

It is said in the spiritual writings such as the Upanishad that you should pray always for the welfare of all and not for yourself alone. If you pray for all, you are inevitably included in that. This fact is rarely followed or practiced and is often forgotten. This is really sad. We seem to have an inbuilt preference for ourselves. Howsoever honest a devotee may be, he/she usually wants a boon for self and not for the welfare of all. They forget that for the Supreme we are all alike and deserve its grace equally. Our actions are like one son or daughter demanding everything from the father denying his benevolence to our brothers and sisters. This is unfair, to say the least.

Universal outlook is a sign of our maturity as humans. It is also a sign of our spiritual growth. The higher we are advanced as spiritual beings, the more universal in outlook we become.

Lastly, I can only say, may the Supreme One give us wisdom to appreciate this fact and inspire us to follow the interest of whole humanity and not seek our interest alone.

15
UNIVERSAL OUTLOOK

Science has shown that energy and matter are interrelated and the relation is mathematically formulated into Einstein's famous equation where mass multiplied by square of the velocity of light equals energy. All matter in the universe has its origin in the creative energy. And that is the ultimate reality.

In Hindu religious philosophy, the ultimate reality is considered conscious energy depicted by the dual image of Shiva and Parvati, Shiva symbolizing consciousness and Parvati representing the material aspect. The two are shown in Ardhnarishwar form, conveying the concept in image form. The two aspects, consciousness and matter or energy, are inseparable like the two sides of a coin. This constitutes the ultimate reality. According to this view, all matter is believed to have the consciousness embedded into it. In living matter such as the humans, the consciousness is apparent while in the nonliving matter it is dormant.

The universal form of consciousness is the Supreme consciousness or the Super-consciousness which is believed to be the ultimate cause of all visible universe. It appears as the creative energy and manifests itself in all forms of material objects in the universe. However, as science has shown, not all energy at the big bang stage appears as the visible matter. In fact it is only about five percent. The rest is dark energy and dark matter that is still not fully understood and remains a subject of research. The point of all this is that it is energy that is the true reality of everything in the universe.

It is the creative energy that is manifested in us as a collection of atoms, chemical molecules and bio-molecules through the process of evolution. In its universal form the energy is spread vast, almost to infinite extent, while in human form it is constrained to finite small space. The same applies to consciousness. The super--consciousness is infinite, eternal, and present everywhere. In human form it is confined to a small finite extent.

In spiritual effort, we try to extend our consciousness to larger dimensions. The expansion of human consciousness is thus an intentional effort, the ultimate goal being to merge it in the infinite Super-consciousness. It would be like a river merging into the vast ocean and losing its identity in that.

Super-consciousness embodied in human form is the soul that is behind the functioning of every part of the body. It is believed to be the sense of the human senses. As the Upanishads say, it is the eye of the eye, ear of the ear and so on.

The spiritual growth is the process of expanding human consciousness to ever growing dimensions. In human body, Super-consciousness, confined in the form of soul, is restricted to the limits of the human consciousness. Our efforts at spiritualizing ourselves are therefore an expression of universalizing our thoughts and actions. As we grow in spirituality, we start thinking of the interests of larger humanity than merely self-serving our interests. That is why we find saints and spiritual masters engaging in activities like delivering discourses and preaching and practicing universal interests like organizing agencies for the help of the poor and the needy. Just as Shri Vivekananda founded the

Ramakrishna Mission for spreading spiritual awareness among masses, so the spiritual gurus even today are organizing centers of help for the benefit of common people. This is because they genuinely feel the plight of others. This is not only found in one religion but in other religions too. The intentions of the organizers are pure but, like anywhere else, deviations and aberrations do appear due to self-interests of the followers.

The point I am making is that spiritually high persons develop a genuine urge to serve globally and do it as part of their spiritual duty. Universal outlook therefore is a characteristic indication of one's spiritual bent of mind, provided of course, there is no personal interest involved. Politicians too work for common people but their self-interest distinguishes them from genuine spiritual persons. Desire for helping others arises basically from an inner urge to be useful to society and treating everybody equal. The helping one considers all as brothers and sisters and children of the same Supreme Being. This tendency to help others selflessly is a spiritual trait. As I said earlier, the sages of olden times considered the whole humanity as one big family. This feeling arose from their spiritual training and practice and became indicative of their good social behavior in thought and deeds.

From the point of view of right living, having a universal outlook in life is a plus point. It is so because it is a spiritual quality. Caring and concern for others, especially all humanity irrespective of man-made divisions, makes a person have a touch of divinity. It is like the concern that the Almighty has for its creation. Such a quality in a person implies love for all, and love is a noble sentiment. People consider love for all a quality that all humans must have. But in practice, it is rarely adopted and followed except by those who have risen above the mundane negative emotions and have expanded their consciousness to global limits. The universal love is expected to cover not only humans but all living species which form part of nature's creation.

***

Philanthropy

Philanthropy and charity are positive qualities that people expect in good people. These qualities arise from a basic concern for the welfare of others. As such these qualities should be sought and practiced by a person interested in right living. But we must suitably distinguish between charity and philanthropy. Charity has a touch of sympathy while philanthropy has a step higher. In charity we remove the immediate distress of a person by giving help in cash or kind out of sympathy with the needy. In philanthropy the help is provided on a larger scale for improving the poor and needy status of an individual or a group of people or even an organization. To be a philanthropist one must have sufficient resources and a will to improve the society. He/she can then share his/her wealth with those whose need of money or resources is greater than that of his/her own.

Benevolent nature is not necessarily a function of the affluence of a person. There are very wealthy people in this world who stick to their wealth like glue to paper. It is near impossible to extract a small sum from them to help the poor and needy. Their life's mission is how to make money from others. Sharing is not in their blood. On the other hand, there are people in this world who would easily part with large sums for creating institutions for putting people on their feet. They will create educational institutions, hospitals, research institutes, orphanages and old peoples' homes and fund them continuously to benefit the society. I particularly admire those who create technical training institutions to train young people for making their careers. This not only benefits the young graduates but also the country at large since skilled persons are the real wealth of any country. This improves the economy and pulls the country out of morass of poverty and backwardness.

Philanthropists are an asset for any society. They may be within the country or outside the country. There are some global philanthropists who make a name for themselves by creating global research institutions whose purpose s to enhance the knowledge of the whole humanity. Such organizations work for the new technology and create fundamental breakthroughs to take the whole world a step higher in knowledge and prosperity.

It is a fact that money drives the world. But to use that money for lifting the poor and needy is a highly noble and even spiritual act. Money is after all made from people. It is therefore right that some of it must be fed back to the people to benefit them. Many religious books on codes of conduct prescribe that a fixed percentage of your earning must be spent for the welfare of the poor and the needy. Generally, it is between one sixth and one sixteenth of your income. But what really matters is the spirit of sharing your resources with those who desperately need help to alleviate their misery. It is a very sad sight to watch people squandering their money on useless items of enjoyment or even harmful things of consumption and not sparing a penny for the needy ones.

Basically, philanthropy is to promote common good and improve the quality of life. Donation in general is given to people or organizations for various purposes. It is given for religious reasons to earn religious merit, to political parties for self-gain, to welfare organizations such as orphanages and old age homes, to teaching and training institutes as scholarships and financial support for running the institutes, to community centers for entertainment and so on. In my opinion however, support to education sector is most important as it generates growth of individuals as well as the society and the country. Support could be either as loan or free aid. Donation to religious institutes and organizations has much emotional appeal as well as easing of conscience. Everybody wants to book a seat in heaven for use after death. People with money find it easier to do so by large donations to their favorite religious deity or to the temple famous for granting boon.

Providing free food to hungry people through temples, mosques and gurudwaras is indeed a noble gesture. Feeding people is a virtuous act, provided the intention is selfless and not self-serving. People also give summer and winter clothing that is as good as feeding the people. The whole idea is to help and serve fellow humans as best as one can do.

Some people extend their fellow feeling to animals too. They support organizations that do-good work for the welfare of dogs, cats and cows and so on. As I said earlier, it is not only good to have kind feelings for every human being but it is equally good to have same feeling for other species too. Brotherly feeling for others is a high point of philanthropy.

Providing free medical aid is one of the best ways to do philanthropic work. It is for various reasons. Firstly, it is very costly. Secondly relieving pain is one the noblest work. Thirdly large numbers of people need this service. No doubt government of the local or central administration provides free hospitals but they are always overcrowded and have bureaucratic hassles. Also, some people build hospitals for providing medical aid to common people but the charges for some services like diagnostic tests are prohibitively high which defeats the philanthropic purpose. The argument put forward by private hospitals is that their running costs are very high. But this actually is the point. Philanthropy needs to give aid to those who are not in a position to bear high cost of medical aid. If the private hospitals are prohibitively costly the poor and the needy cannot afford it and the purpose of philanthropy is lost to them.

There is another side to religious philanthropy. People who make temples and shelter houses for common public put advertising stone tablets telling to the people that they have done philanthropic work. This is an expression of their ego and defeats the purpose of selfless work. They should know that only selfless work is spiritual. Any expression of ego defeats that purpose.

Philanthropy is good but intention must be honest and selfless. At least that is so for right living.

16
Live and Let Live

The above expression essentially means that we must avoid violence in our thoughts and deeds, violence to humans, animals living on earth and under water, birds, insects, plants and any other living beings that either too weak or too slam to face our might. This kind of nonviolence is a creed with some religions like Jainism and Buddhism where it is the highest Dharma.

In earlier days violence was largely physical in nature, but today there are various ways in which we inflict violence on others physically as well as mentally. We think ill of others. We cheat and cause economic harm in more ways than one. We forcibly thrust our views and beliefs on others. We induce temptations in the minds of others that may harm them and so on.

Centuries ago, the invaders and colonialists looted, and killed for self-gain. That practice however, has faded and almost become extinct. But the habit of making money by exploiting others still exists. It is done through economic and technical domination. There are business men and women who will not hesitate to make unduly large profits by selling their goods to the poor and needy persons and governments by using their monopoly in the market. This is economic violence and is as wrong as physical violence. The sale of arms and ammunition to warring groups is also a kind of violence because ultimately it kills people.

Politicians do not hesitate to create enmity between people and nations for their benefit. This is also a form of violence, though a sophisticated one. Threats and punishment to innocent people from law enforcement agencies is also a kind of violence, though it is nicely garbed in the guise of maintenance of law and order.

The evolved human brain with its power of intellect has found many new ways to inflict violence on some other species by naming them as harmful to human existence. Mighty people still want to grab, by hook or crook, resources of the weak and poor, resources that are essential to their survival. They call might is right as law of nature. But saints and prophets have always strongly condemned this tendency. Religion has always supported the poor and the weak by advising the people to live and let live.

Violence is just one aspect of human behavior that denies others their right to life. Denial of sharing of nature's resources is another. Here greed plays its part. At individual as well as collective level, people today want much more than what their basic needs are. This causes deprivation of large number of people. It results in friction in society and later comes out in the form of social turbulence and even violence.

Modern way of life rests on production and consumption. The two are obviously interrelated in the sense that more consumption needs more production. When desires are created and they outnumber the needs, the consumption-based society becomes exploitive and wasteful. This is the economic pattern that most countries are following today. This is harmful to nature and harmful to individual as well. Nature's resources get depleted fast and consumer becomes unhealthy and fat. This is obviously not the right way to live because this is unnatural and ultimately destructive for other living species in nature.

One may well ask how 'live and let live 'principle is related to right living. The link is established by the fact that right living should not affect adversely the life of others. In fact, right living person must feel concern for others' difficulties and should have empathy for all. This is what 'live and let live' principle implies.

Wealth gives power and power generates arrogance of superiority. This is especially true if the wealth is accumulated through greed and unethical means. As I stated earlier, lack of ethics takes a person away from right living.

Some people want to grow tall by riding on the shoulders of others. This is a wrong way of self-improvement. Every success must come from individual's own efforts with sincerity, honesty and hard work. One may take however some help from others in specific situations but with the strict stipulation that this help in no way causes any inconvenience or harm to the helper. To ignore someone's inconvenience and even plight in the interest of self-gain is just not right. It is worse if it is gained by force of threat or pressure of dominance.

Everyone has a different level of expressing ego. Some take pleasure in causing difficulty to others and think themselves smart enough to do so. This is obviously a form of sadistic behavior. Others are compelled by their wrong conditioning to behave badly with others. Some, out of ignorance or lack of education, want to show off their power and cause suffering to others. Expression of ego therefore, is also responsible for others' miserable state. The sufferers are especially those who, out of modesty or respect for human values, do not react violently to the egoists. Their gentleness and cultured background is seen as weakness by the wrong doers.

Denial of freedom to others is also a form of violating the principle of live and let live. This often happens when the powerful one is afraid of others' rise to his/her status. In many cases this sort of behavior is shown by cowardly people who are afraid of others' power. Sometimes it is expressed as non-acceptance of others' views and suggestions.

Generally, the wrong doers refuse to play with society's rules and codes of conduct because that dents their ego. They even dishonor and disrespect the responsible members of home and society. When questioned they make fun of others' rights ignore their own responsibilities. Tyranny of abusive and untruthful behavior is also a major cause of people's discomfort with such bad eggs in society.

Lastly I can only give hope to people by saying that do not under rate the power of love, especially the power of loving all. It takes a person a few notches high in spiritual growth.

***

You are Never Alone

If you think you can commit a wrong thing in thought or action without being seen by anyone, you are mistaken. This is because you are always under the watchful eyes of the Supreme Being. As stated earlier, the Supreme one in the form of Super-consciousness is present everywhere in the universe and a part of it sits in every heart as soul. Another way of saying this is that God sits in every heart and is always aware of all your actions, whether you are among the people, in front of the recording device or simply sitting at home or in an isolated place without any physical being watching you.

The Karma theory tells us that every action of ours has a reaction and we reap the crop of actions as we sow them. This is possible only when all our actions are recorded at some level and accounted for. Therefore, think before you do anything wrong, like cheating or deceiving anyone. You are being watched for not only your actions but for your intentions as well. This is the reason, in my opinion, why crimes committed in total absence of any witness get ultimately detected and punished for.

There is a proverbial saying that you cannot hide anything from the Supreme One. This saying must prevent people to do wrong things when they are physically alone. But the human nature being what it is, a person only believes what he sees with his eyes. The Supreme one, that is witness to all our actions, and present everywhere, is not visible to our physical eyes. Therefore, we do not believe the saying. Also, some people do not have any faith in the Karma theory. That is the reason people keep doing wrong things unhesitatingly, without any fear of being caught, when they are alone.

Whether one believes in the above saying or not, it is good to abide by the intention behind it because no society accepts wrong doing either by an atheist or by a religious one.

17
Practices of Spirituality

It was summer evening. The sun had gone down the horizon and the light was getting duskier. Two cots were placed under a shady tree. The dusty ground had been sprinkled with water. It was giving the sweet smell of wet earth. Five men, in the later part of their life, were sitting on the cots. These men came every evening and chatted till it was dark. One was from a house where a new life was born a day earlier while another one came from the house where his father had expired only two weeks back. The other three came from adjoining houses. The gathering of five had been friendly from last ten years and this was their daily routine. A cool breeze had started flowing and this made them comfortable and chatty.

After sitting silent for a while, one of them broke the silence and said, 'today I was thinking what a strange life we all live. We toil hard every year, raise crops with our sweat and yet we cannot afford to acquire the things that make life comfortable and pleasant as city people do. From birth to death this is our life.' While he was going on his grumble game, another one intervened and said,' you are particularly unfortunate because your land does not yield as much as that of others. Don't worry, comfort and enjoyment is not all that life has to offer. There is disease, agony and suffering also in everyone's life.

The city people also have their share of discomfort because they live in unhealthy environment. We at least live in fresh air and are healthier than most city people. The third one said, 'let us not talk about comfort and misery. There is much more than that in life. You have a chance to do well to others and that makes your life worthwhile to live as a human being. If nature is kind or cruel, it is for all and we have no ground to consider only ourselves as unfortunate.'

Before he could say anything more, the fourth one intercepted and said,' tell me if there is any purpose for our living in this world. Many times I think this cycle of birth to death is just meaningless because we keep doing the routine things and then disappear in death. Do we achieve anything special in our life; do we make any mark in society by our presence?

At this point the fifth one could not control him and he said,' don't be so pessimistic. Every life has a purpose. We all add to the economy of the country and abide by the natural laws of sustaining the creation of God. 'It was now the first one who countered the view of the fifth one. He said,' I do not agree we are here for sustaining nature's creation. Nature can look after itself. We are here to eat, drink and be merry. But society has put us in this position to labor and live a hard life.' The second one said,' do not blame the society. If there is anybody who is responsible for our present condition it is our own actions that make our destiny. We very easily forget our past deeds and start blaming God or nature or society for our troubles. You may not believe in the past life but I do. So stop blaming others for your destiny or your problematic life.'

The third one immediately sensed that the talk was becoming controversial, so he said,' look we are not in this life to blame this and that. In my view, our purpose in life is to do good and be good. In this way we shall rise in the eyes of God and we shall be born in such a family that would give us a comfortable time all our life.' The fourth one seemed to agree and said,' I think we should be religious and pious and caring for others. That is why I go to temple twice a day, I daily pray to God and I am helpful to my co-workers. This claim to goodness made the fifth one say,' it is alright if you go to temple but is it the only way to be good. Do you have any knowledge of spirituality, the human values of life and are you truly conscious of your inner self? It is both knowledge and practice of spirituality that counts in your religious merit.' The fifth was in the mood to go on but the first one saw a swami go past him. He immediately addressed him and said,' swami ji, please enlighten us about the purpose of life and the spiritual techniques that can improve our life.' The swami was both amused and surprised at this request. But he controlled his emotions and said,' brothers, I was going for my evening prayers in the temple in the nearby village. But I have some time at my disposal. Therefore, I will comply with your request. Maybe it will satisfy you.'

The swami then sat comfortably on the cot and said,' everyone has a set purpose in life, at least those who care to set a purpose. You all know some live for enjoyment, some decide to rob and cheat while others do social service. Some consider raising children and educating them as their main purpose of life. There are some religious people who decide to renounce their life and they either live like a mendicant or join some religious order. Some believe in heaven and hell and try to remain on the right side of their deity. But I will tell you what the spiritualists think as the purpose of life. According to them, our life is a chance given by nature to improve our Karma and ensure spiritual growth so that ultimately, we would raise ourselves enough to become enlightened and join the Super-consciousness, the reality of all beings in the universe. Your inner light or the soul needs to be uncovered from the thick covering of bad Karma so that it can shine bright within you. In my view, the aim of life is to attain the spiritual goal so that you are freed from the cycle of birth and death. Generally, for common people, this task is not easy. It requires strong will, high level of determination, an enlightened guru to guide and lifelong meditation on the Supreme Being. Very few people can do all this and therefore, they remain entangled in the web of birth and death. Hence, they suffer the consequences of their actions life after life. Since most people do wrong actions under temptations, greed and undesirable wants and emotions, they undergo sufferance and then curse their destiny, forgetting that they themselves made their destiny.'

Scriptures have however described the purpose of life by stating it has four components which everyone must comply with. The first is to learn and protect dharma, the second is to earn wealth, the third to fulfill desires and fourth and most important to seek salvation. Based on these four parts the life period was also divided into four parts; the first part was education, the second and third parts for making a family and performing the duties of a householder, the last part for study of scriptures, leaving the family connection and meditate for attaining salvation. Thus the scriptures also emphasize the importance of working for attaining the ultimate goal of spirituality, namely trying to use this life for attaining salvation or liberation from the cycle of birth and death.

The swami then took a deep breath, thought for a moment and said,' now I come to your second question about how to practice spirituality. In Hindu religion there is full freedom to choose the way you want to spiritualize yourself. For example, either of the three methods or the three methods together as described in Bhagwadgita can be practiced. These methods are the knowledge and meditation, devotion, and selfless work as are widely known to people who are conversant with the message of Bhagwadgita. The methods are suited to different types of people such as intellectual, emotional and physical work-oriented. Hinduism in fact is a democratic religion and everyone has the choice to adopt any form of God's image and worship it. It is based on the belief that God resides in every being though there is no specific form to describe it. It is formless and yet all forms originate from it. Therefore, if you are interested in meditating on its form, you could choose anyone of the images and concentrate on it. People take a painted stone or an image on paper for this purpose and consider it as God and meditate on it. Some yogis use a point or the tip of a flame to concentrate for meditative purpose. As I said, you only need an object to concentrate your mind on it. As for concentration, you could do it by worship method or the yogic meditation depending on your capacity and personal preference. All it takes is sincere devotion and repeated practice with clean heart and ethical and moral living. The life style should be simple. By simple I mean not running after the attractions of senses. For example, simple food with not too much spicy content, no greed, no gaudy taste in appearance and behavior.

The reason for going to temple is that it provides an atmosphere conducive to concentrating on God. You could even make your own temple at home and create an environment for meditative silence. Of course, you need the help of a guru if you are going for advanced meditation. It is up to you to choose the right guru depending on your confidence in him/her to guide you properly.

Another method is to repeatedly recite with the help of a rosary either the name of God or any mantra given by the guru. This is commonly called in Sanskrit as Jap yoga and it is quite easy to practice, provided in doing so your mind does not waver from one thought to another frequently. If it does so, you may ignore the disturbing thought and revert to the name or the mantra without any sense of guilt. Meditation and Jap yoga are practiced in other religions too. Bhagwadgita gives great importance to this Jap yoga. The postural yoga, which is a part of Hath yoga, is for maintaining good health. But Hath yoga as such is a rigorous spiritual practice used by yogis of earlier as well as present time.

Rituals and mythological tales add to the religious fervor and help you to stay your thoughts on God. The test of spiritual growth is how much your practice has improved your inner self. It should be reflected in your ethical and moral behavior and the strength of your belief in the Supreme Power. I suggest you must devote at least half an hour each morning and evening in the pursuit of God's grace.

The study of religious scriptures gives additional benefit since they strengthen your spiritual thoughts about your ultimate reality and clear your doubts about the existence of God's forms and their significance in spiritual practice. As is well known, religious practice involves spirituality in thought and action, rituals for bodily involvement in the service of the Supreme One, and mythology for admiring the power of God. Spirituality is essentially based on the religious philosophy about the existence of the Supreme Being. Its practice is universally related to meditation on the Supreme One. It may take the form of prayer, meditation, visiting the religious places to hear discourses and strengthening the belief on right living. Overall, it is a method to improve oneself by feeling the power of the inner light.

Practice of spirituality improves thought mechanism. It clears the garbage and purifies thought process. It improves one's intuitive thinking; belief in the invisible universal power gives inner strength. All these qualities are helpful to our power to handle worldly problems that disturb us mentally and physically day in and day out.'

Saying this, the swami stopped and said that it was time for him to leave since people must be waiting for him to do the evening worship of the deity in the temple. The five also thought it was getting dark and it was time for them too to leave for home, otherwise their family members would worry about them and may start searching for them. Thus, came to stop the discussion on the purpose of life and the method of practicing spirituality.

***

Why Don't I See God?

A long time ago there was a village of some hundred persons on the bank of a river. A kilometer away, there was the edge of a forest through which the river flowed. The villagers were farmers who had their lands nearby. The river met the requirements of water both for the villagers and their lands. The environment was clean and the forest fulfilled the basic necessities of food, water and shelter for the animal life living there. It also provided the firewood to the villagers who depended on it on a daily basis. The village of course had its share of trees and plants too.

One day a stranger came to the village and settled himself under the great banyan tree that adorned the village scene. The stranger cleaned the place, put his scanty belongings there and sat down to meditate. However, what attracted the attention of the villagers was that he did not require anything from the villagers for three days and still managed on his own. Some villagers became curious to find out how he managed to live without food and did nothing but meditate day and night.

One day one villager decided to find out. He went to the place where the stranger was in meditation and waited for him to open his eyes. After about half an hour, the stranger opened his eyes and asked the villager what he wanted. The villager told him the purpose of his visit and asked him why he did not eat anything for the upkeep of his body. The stranger smiled and said,' for me, eating is not a priority, though I do eat whenever I become hungry. I rely on the fruit of this tree which you think is not worth eating. When there is no fruit from this tree, I will pluck a few leaves from any tree and eat. That satisfies my hunger and I take the water from the river. My needs of food, water and shelter are thus fulfilled by this tree and the river. I have come to this place to complete my spiritual goal which I vowed to do at a young age. Please do not worry about my needs as these are met by God who is the provider for all.'

'How can you talk about God as the provider when He is invisible and we do not know whether He exists?' said the villager. 'Can you see the air when you know it exists?' said the stranger. 'We know it exists because we can feel its presence when we breathe, and also when the leaves move because of its movement.' replied the villager. 'That is exactly the point. Even though you cannot see the invisible you can infer its presence by its effect on material things. You cannot see God because your eyes are not capable to see Him. But you can certainly feel His presence through the effect He has on your body and mind and also on every bit of creation.' said the stranger. 'Have you seen Him or felt His presence?' asked the villager. 'Yes, I can feel His presence all around me; in the growth of plants and trees, in the sunshine, wind and rain, in the mountains, rivers, in the laughter of children and the toils of people for survival. Have you not observed the seeds sprouting in the field? How can you ignore His power when He gives you a good yield from a handful of seeds? His power is observable in all activities in the world. You cannot see Him because He does not have a fixed shape or form. He is the infinite and eternal intelligent energy or what we call as the Supreme Power residing in all beings and things; from an atom to the biggest star. He is the power behind our senses. It is the limited capability of our senses that we cannot see this power directly. But we know crops grow because of this power, a child grows from childhood to old age because of this power, volcanoes and storms in sea show His power, celestial bodies and astronomical objects follow their paths because of this power. In fact, nothing moves without His will and everything in the universe is in motion because of His power.' said the stranger.

'But how is it that you see His power and I don't? The villager was rather perplexed by the words of the stranger. 'Oh, it is because you have not yet developed the keen vision or the special eyes to see His supreme and universal presence. As they say, you must have the knowledge eyes to see and feel His closeness to you. But I assure you, you have the power to observe Him and you can develop special eyes through the spiritual practices that our sages have prescribed. There is no cause for despair. If you are interested, I can show you the way to have a firsthand feel of the presence of God.' The stranger stopped at this point to see the reaction of the villager.

The perplexed villager was now beginning to give respect to the stranger and he thought, may be, he was face to face with a noble soul. He therefore said,' May be sir, you have trained your mind and body for having special eyes through rigorous spiritual practices. But for a common man, I believe, it is not so easy to see the power of God. '

'No, you are de-rating yourself. Everybody has the power, inherent but latent, in him to develop special eyes. But unfortunately, they have spread a cover of their Karma round the inner light within. If you meditate regularly, you can also remove that cover and your inner vision will shine and you will see the Divine Light. Many illiterates but determined persons have achieved this miracle in their life, what one can do, you can do also. Only your determination is required. If you follow the path, the Supreme Guide will take you along the path and will show you the destination. But you have to walk the path yourself

At this point the villager said,' Sir, I don't disbelieve you. But the whole exercise seems to be very difficult since I see you following a very strict regimen; living the life of a secluded one and spending hours in meditation. We villagers have to look after our families and cannot isolate ourselves the way you have done.' 'No, to feel God you don't have to go that far. Remaining in the family, you can also move sufficiently on the spiritual path, provided you have the urge or the will to do so. You may start by spending an hour or so in the remembrance of the Supreme Power and develop unbreakable faith in His universal presence. Slowly and slowly, your thoughts will get purified and one day you will see the light. But I leave it to you to change your lifestyle. Clear your heart and mind of all evil thoughts and decide to lead a simple life, believing in the goodness of man and his desire to reach the heights of divinity. Abandon all thoughts of selfishness, untruthfulness, cruelty and deception and try to see God in every human being and in all things around you. If you can do this much in this life, you have achieved a lot.'

With these words, the stranger stopped and the villager took leave of him. While going home, the villager kept thinking about the stranger and his way of life and wondered whether it was worth all the effort that he was making to experience God.

18
Learning from the Lives of the Good and the Great

Every day we work and do actions that invite comments from people, some sweet and some sour. This applies to a right living person too. It is in the nature of humans to appreciate or criticize depending on their view of what is right and what is wrong. At the same time there are some rules of conduct that are universally accepted as desirable and some actions that are not so desirable. Speaking the truth, caring for others, doing actions that help others are some of the desirable traits in a person. Siding with evil, speaking ill of others without any basis, trying to harm others in self-interest are some of the undesirable acts.

How do we mold our life so that we do more of good than otherwise? One of the ways to improve ourselves is to learn others plus points. This requires a keen sense of observation and critical assessment of the results of others' actions. One could also search the written word and get inspiration from the good and great lives that have gone by.

There is a large amount of literature available, practically in all societies that enlighten us about the ideals that we must follow as examples, ideals that have been shown by the great leaders and thinkers in every era, right from Vedic times to the recent past. We learn from religious books, the stories from Puranas, the biographies of sages, the epics like Ramayana and Mahabharata, the shrutis and Smritis, the great thinkers like the ones who wrote the six Shastras and so on. There is indeed no dearth of advice and examples presented to us by the great ones. But the tragedy is that in spite of all this, most of us listen and forget, or even completely ignore the words of wisdom and go on living the wrong way simply guided by self-interest and following the instinct of survival.

The idealist way, though difficult, shines bright as a beacon to show the people the right way to live with spirituality as an important component of life. This is the way of the spiritualists, the yogis and the sages. This is the way that has been pointed out in religious literature and has been practiced for centuries. People found happiness in their life by its practice and they preached it to others. But with changes in social structures and circumstances of living over the period, it became so difficult to follow this path that people needed an alternative. People moved to city life and preferred comfort to the hard life of an idealist. But this comfort and easy way of life was a mirage. Chasing happiness in an easier life proved unrealistic. The comfortable life brought illness, diseases and indulgences of various sorts. People therefore needed a way of life that easy and yet free from sufferings and discomfort. Some thinking persons, like the great Buddha, experimented with their life and found a middle path. They preached it to people and advised them to limit their desires if they were really interested in happiness. Also, they had to spend a part of their waking hours to practice meditation. This was a path that combined spirituality with working life. This was indeed the middle path where the idealist and the practical way of life combined together to attain the desired happiness without giving away one for the other. Later on, many illustrious spiritual leaders promoted and advocated it to people and said they could lead a normal family life and at the same time continue spiritual practices like meditation in order to get happiness in their life. In a way they combined the outward life with the inner reality of man so as to derive benefit of both. They emphasized that inner awakening was necessary for attaining happiness. The present spiritual gurus also advise us the same pattern of life. In this way, one lives an ethical and moral life with spiritual study and practice and also performs the worldly duties of normal life. This gives the realization that the source of happiness lies within us and not outside.

There are still some persons who go for strict idealist way but they are now a small minority among the large population that wants comfortable modern life of technology and wealth and also needs mental peace and emotional health. That is the modern right living pattern where a person enjoys family life and also goes for inner source of happiness by following the idealist's pattern of meditation and austerity.

Why does the unhappiness arise in the practical way of life? I think it is basically due to the presence of evil in society. It exists in various forms. The idealist left the practical worldly way and went alone in far away from the society, and thereby escaped the clutches of evil. The family man who lives in society cannot do so because of his duties to the family. He therefore has to face the evil ways of people.

In different times people have devised ways to fight the evil in society. In earlier times the king, and now the democratic governments, take up the fight against evil by setting up mechanisms for it. But the laxity in implementation of these mechanisms still allow evil to cause problems to people. One of the ways to fight evil in society is to spread spirituality among the people. Whenever spirituality fades from the life of people, evil spreads its wings wider and suffering enters the lives of people. Right living has been, and is today also, the desired thing to do to make society worth living.

From earliest times, people have sought instructions from the wise persons in society for living right. There are of course some other sources for wise sayings too. One of these sources is the mythological stories written in religious books from Vedic times. These stories advise us in symbolical form the great truths of life. One of the famous ones is about the churning of sea by the gods and anti-gods for getting invaluable assets in their lives. The prime motive for this was of course the obtaining of elixir of life for attaining immortality. As a result of churning there appeared from the sea the great god of medicine, the goddess of wealth, an urn containing poison and lastly the much sought after the elixir of life. The idea seems to convey firstly that sea is a great source of invaluable products that are useful to our life. But I see this story in a different way. To me it conveys symbolically the great message about the role of thoughts in our life. I must say it is my interpretation which may or may not agree with generally accepted version of the story. I consider the sea as the symbol of the vast source of thoughts that portray the positive and negative tendencies represented by the gods and anti-gods. The churning of thoughts leads to the poisonous effects as well as the means of obtaining wealth and knowledge like the curing of the body and mind. Both positive and negative tendencies seek immortality the elixir of life. The great benefactors like the spiritual masters soak up the poisonous elements from the society as the great yogi Shiva did in the story. There is both benefit and disaster hidden in the sea of thoughts so churn the thoughts properly in order to get the benefit and not the harm to self or society. It is our thoughts that have the capacity to make or mar our life.

There is another tale of of the Vedic era in which the sage Daddhichi gives his bones to the king of gods to make a weapon so as to defeat the anti-gods the anti-god represents the dark side of human life. The sacrifice of the sage represents the chi valorous virtue of giving life for the protection of society from bad elements. Such incidences inspire confidence in the goodness of man. It helps even the divine to fight evil and save the human race. It is a great example of selflessness that is rarely seen in the modern era.

There is another story from the truthful era called the Satyug. It is almost proverbial to talk of king Harishchandra who suffered endless problems to defend the truth. He was tested for his stand on truthfulness by the sage Vishvamitra in a number of incidents where the king had to undergo many hardships to stick to truth. The story highlights the fact that it is not easy to walk on the path of truth in our life. But ultimately, as the Vedas say, it is truth that triumphs. Similarly, the king after suffering many setbacks, including the break- up of his family, he came out successful in upholding the path of truth.

When I talk of messages from the mythological tales, I am not concerned with the debates about the truth or otherwise of happenings. I am only concerned with the positive messages the stories convey to me. In all this study of the religious literature, I believe, this must be the approach. It should be to learn the positive messages that the stories convey and not fight or bicker about

The great epics Ramayana and Mahabharata present a number of ideals for the common man and that is the reason of their popularity among the masses. A theme that is common to both the stories is that it is advisable to avoid violent confrontation with evil by first persuasion and wise counsel. But if the evil persists and refuses to listen to reason then violent action has to be resorted to in order to finish evil. In such situations violence is justified to finish evil. But it is not justified to perpetrate it on innocent victims. The brave and the good characters of the epics, though small in numbers compared to the large armies of the enemy, prevailed over them because truth was on their side. Divine power also sides with the truth. That is why the Upanishad proclaims that truth always triumphs. The evil may give initially some setbacks but, in the end, it is truth that wins.

To be specific, Ramayana teaches us many lessons. Firstly, it displays extraordinary obedience to parents. Rama went to exile for fourteen years willingly in order to honor the promise of his father. He accepted the sufferings of forest life while refusing the throne of Ayodhya. Such a great sacrifice is rare among people. While in forest, he helped the sages by fighting the evil intruders into the peaceful life of the meditating sages. Even in extreme adversity, when his wife was stolen, he did not lose his cool and used his wisdom and bravery to create an army to fight the evil on its own ground. It is no small task for a lonely person living in the forest with his brother and facing the onerous task of fighting a strong evil force. Lastly, when he defeated the enemy he did not annex the territory but willingly gave it to the noble relative of the evil king. His rule in Ayodhya is proverbially known as the best ever. He gave peace and prosperity to all his subjects and ruled with justice and fairness towards all. The love between the brothers of Rama is another example of right living. The sacrifice of Laxman and Bharat's loyalty to Rama are worthy of admiration and praise even today.

Krishna's life presented an example of tactful handling of evil persons. His whole life was devoted to helping the poor and needy and support for the noble-minded persons. He too fought the evil and defeated it wherever it existed. His role in

Mahabharata is central to the theme of victory of goodness over evil. Krishna's address to the warrior Arjuna provides wisdom of high order that is sacred to all Hindus. The message of Bhagwadgita is indeed universal and an ideal for all humanity.

Another king of eminence, whose tales of good rule are legendry, was Vikramaditya. He gave peace and prosperity to people, ruled with justice and kindness and presented an example of how to rule and still win the hearts of people. He was the one who created the Hindu calendar of Vikrami Samvat starting from 57 B.C. This calendar is still in vogue in the Hindu system of dating the events. He was a symbol of valor, wisdom and care for those who depended on him for sustenance. People still remember him with admiration for his golden period of peace, plenty, freedom and encouragement to arts and growth of spiritual awareness. It is believed there was no king equal to him for a long period before or after him.

Hindu way of life, emphasizing ethics and morality in behavior and spiritual inclination for seeking peace of mind has been in existence for a long time, though for some time it saw ups and downs due to invasions of alien cultures. But in all this it has retained the essential element of Vedanta thought as the basic philosophy of spiritual awareness. Maharishi Ved Vyas was the great sage who put Vedanta on firm footing. He had a school of learned sages who wrote a number of books to create a sound foundation to Hindu religious thought. Mahabharata and many Puranas like Bhagwat carry stories which promote the philosophy of Vedanta and pious living. In later times it was the great saint philosopher Adi Shankaracharya who carried forward the tradition of Vedanta. His contribution is all the more significant because in a short span of life he travelled to all the corners of the country and established four centers of Hindu culture which are in existence even today. His commentaries on religious texts are praise worthy. He gave a new life to Hindu religious thought at a time when it was getting under cloud of alternate religions. His sharp and brilliant intellect could defeat the great thinkers of that time. His life is an inspiration for all spiritual seekers today.

In the recent past, specifically the last two centuries, two great spiritual leaders reawakened people's interest in spirituality by their spiritual power. Swami Ramakrishna Paramhans worshipped the deity in a temple and attained great spiritual power through total devotion and simple life. Similarly, Sri Raman Maharishi meditated at Arunachala and gained great spiritual status. Both the luminaries are highly respected by people for their achievement as great spiritual masters. They led the masses to the path of spirituality and pious living. Their spiritual attainment was an example to the common man. It showed that given the determination and continuous spiritual practice, it is possible to achieve the highest spiritual goal. They reawakened common people's interest in spirituality at a time when the alien rule had subdued the freedom and spiritual energy of masses under foreign domination. They gave a new life and new hope to the seekers of spiritual goal. They gave them the confidence that the goal, though difficult, can be achieved as they did in their life.

The task of spreading spiritual awareness was further taken up by Sri Vivekananda and Sri Aurobindo. They encouraged the youth of the country to tread the path of knowledge and spiritual practice. They wrote at length for the literate audience and spread the message of the great sages among the common people. Their role in spiritual awakening in the country is indeed laudable.

I have so far talked about only the spiritual greats of Hindu spiritual tradition. But I am sure; there are examples of good and great personalities in other religions too. We know there have been spiritual leaders and saints in other religions that are highly respected by the common people today. Similarly, even in present age there are many spiritual leaders and teachers doing great work in the service of humanity in all religions. As I said earlier, for a spiritually great person, there is no distinction between one man and another. They do good to all without prejudices and preferences. They bring knowledge and spiritual awareness to all and show the right path to everyone who cares to listen to them.

***

Avoiding Wrong Environment

It is always important to have good friends at every stage of life, be it childhood, youth or old age. By good I mean good at heart, good at speech and good in behavior. It is because we proverbially know that one is judged by the company one keeps. If we move around people with doubtful character, we put our reputation at stake. The reputation and character of our friends inevitably rubs on us if we frequently interact with such persons and do not take precautions to keep ourselves isolated from their wrong doings.

For right living, we require right environment for our growth into a responsible person. Our ignoring this fact may result in negating many of our positive efforts to become a good citizen of society. It is widely known that others' views, ideas and actions have an effect on our mind even if we do not want to adopt them. It has an involuntary side effect on us through the input from our senses even if we intend to remain careful to remain unaffected.

Most wrong habits start at the age when our mind is vulnerable to suggestions by friends and colleagues. Smoking and drinking start in the company of friends at the vulnerable stage, initially out of curiosity. When they become habits, it becomes difficult to get rid of them because they become an integral part of our way of life. It is important that parents keep a watch of their children at this critical age and present them good examples by their own actions and behavior.

Good friends are good advisors too. It is because they have the welfare of their friends at heart. But a spoiled one cares little about what happens to others. He/she is mainly interested in his/her self-interest and personal benefit. A bad apple has the capacity to spoil many other apples kept near it. This is nature's lesson to us, but we generally ignore it to our loss and disadvantage.

There are many foul-mouthed bullies in society; in schools and colleges, in working environment and in time-spending colleagues in old age. These bullies want a set of obeying friends that they tend to dominate. They are the worst elements that vitiate the atmosphere around us. It is important to avoid them as best as one can do, otherwise the result is disastrous at a later stage in life.

Many people, especially the young ones, think that they have a strong will and they would come out of a bad habit whenever they want to do so. But this is a mistaken belief since most people lack the will power that is required to quit a bad habit. The result is that they end up in rehab centers, plunging their parents and relatives to great stress and emotional damage. As they say, prevention is better than cure. It is therefore, necessary to avoid a bad environment and escape the consequent problem, a problem that not only affects self but the near and dear ones too.

The best way to avoid the wrong environment of undesirable friends is to cultivate a harmless hobby such as reading or some mind game that helps to sharpen the mind.

What should be the requirement for a person to grow into a right living one? The first requirement is the home where peace and understanding prevails. As a child, the person should get love, good advice and compassionate behavior from everyone in the family, especially the parents whom the child respects and adores them and considers them as role models. If there is any discord or tension between the father and mother, it has direct effect on the development of the child. The quarrelsome atmosphere in the family leads to the neglect of the child and affects its psychology adversely. The violent and rebellious nature of the child often starts from broken homes. It is more relevant in the present age than it was earlier. The lack of mutual understanding and respect for each other between the husband and wife make the child irritated and it starts thinking it is alright to refuse to listen reason. These traits when developed in childhood become a problem in adulthood and the parents suffer the consequences of their own actions. The rigidity in behavior acquired in early years can harm in the working environment where one has to work with others in a team or under the command of a superior colleague. Any advice given to the person at this stage has little effect on him.

The respect for law and belief in the supreme power go a long way in the person's growth at home. It brings certain amount of humility in behavior that is necessary for living amicably with others, both at working environment and in interaction with common people at large. It is always advantageous to keep one's ego under control, otherwise undesirable results may have to be faced. Both for career development and earning respect in society, good personal behavior is important and for this ego must be kept in check.

Too much pampering also affects the normal growth of the child. The child must learn early that all desires cannot be fulfilled in life. The earlier one learns this fact of life the better it is. Otherwise in later life when some desires are not fulfilled the person becomes dejected and even desperate at times. Time also does not remain the same always. Control of desires comes in handy at difficult times and this goes a long way in molding a balanced life.

It is true that you cannot choose your neighbors though you can choose your friends. If you have the misfortune of having undesirable elements in your neighborhood fou have the choice of keeping a social distance from them so as not to be polluted by their style of living.

The need to live in right environment is continuous. One cannot be lax about it at any stage in life. Though good mental training of early days comes in handy to resist undesirable onslaughts in later life, it is preferable to be watchful of bad interactions in working environment, particularly if the affected person happens to be a sensitive one. As far as old age is concerned, it is rather difficult to change habits acquired earlier.

I would sum up by saying that we need to take a few necessary steps to stay in right environment. Firstly, choose friends with care, second be in the company of ethical and spiritual persons as much as is possible and thirdly do not be tempted by the styles of those who care little for others in their behavior and speech. Lastly, perform your duties towards your children by setting examples of right living before them.

19
Life is Sacred

Life is sacred and treat it so because the Supreme Being resides in every living being. Your life owes a debt to nature. Live to pay this debt and do not squander away your life in trivialities. Set a goal or a purpose for your life and use all your energies of body and mind to achieve that. That way you remain engaged properly. Make full use of the gifts of nature. By doing so, you show respect to the Supreme Power and a commitment to yourself. Engaging body and mind in undesirable thoughts and actions is an insult to the dignity of life and the very purpose of creation.

These days many young men and women lose interest in life due to their incapacity to face problems of life. They think of giving up their life as an easy way to get rid of life's difficulties. But that is a negative approach to life. The right way to live is to take life as it comes and face difficulties with courage and fortitude. As an example of this way of life I give below a story of a boy who had lost interest in life but under proper advice regained his confidence to live for the good of self and for others.

There was a young man in mid-twenties who had earned a name as a good football player in his school days as well as in college. He was the star player of the college team when one day a whole mountain of ill luck fell on him. He was playing in a practice match when he clashed with an obstacle and broke his leg. On first appearance, it looked a minor injury but when the x-ray was taken it showed a big crack in the leg. He was then plastered for three months. When the plaster was removed, the bone had joined but not as it should have been. He therefore developed a limp that prevented him to play football in future. It was a shock that shattered him greatly and his whole mental picture of becoming a state player was torn to pieces. As a result, he developed a permanent demeanor of sadness and reserved look. He lost interest in studies and his grades fell by the month. He lost his place in the college team and looked so depressed as if there was nothing left for him to do anymore in life. He failed to qualify for the entrance test for further studies. When his girlfriend knew of his condition, she broke her relationship with him. This added to his bundle of miseries and he looked hopeless and mentally unprepared to take any useful work. Seeing his condition, his parents looked worried and did not know how to get him out of this abyss of grief and sorrow.

One day his father took him to a doctor and asked him what was wrong with his son. He explained to the doctor his strange behavior and asked whether there was anything physically wrong with him. The doctor examined the boy and asked him if he took any sedating drugs. The boy denied and told him that he was not interested in anything of that sort. In fact, he had been an active sportsman but since his accident he was very much missing his old days. He told him that the recent events in his life had made him lose interest in life. The doctor felt that the boy needed psychological advice and told his father so. The father then took the boy to a psychotherapist, who talked to the boy for half an hour and then told his father,' There is nothing wrong with your boy. In fact he is an intelligent boy who only needs a purpose in life. Try to keep him engaged in activities that generate in him desire for doing something substantial. His failure to pursue his sports career has dampened his spirits. Bring a change in his environment and he will be alright once he gets back to doing something that gives him satisfaction. 'This gave a hope to his father but he did not know where and how to engage him. However, the father had a friend who regularly visited a holy place of spiritual seekers. He consulted this friend and was told that he would take the boy to that place when he went there next. His friend hoped that this visit may provide a diversion that the boy needed badly. If the boy listened to the inspiring talk of the head of the holy place, it may inspire the boy to have a purpose in life. The father agreed to the suggestion of his friend and the boy started visiting the holy place, although initially he had some reservations.

Eventually, the boy's interest in discourses increased till one day the head of the place told him,' Life is a sacred gift of nature and it should not be wasted in purposeless pursuits. Human brain is the best creation in the world. Make its use for self-improvement and know yourself the reality of your existence. You must understand that human mind and body have tremendous potential to do things for the good for self and for others. Nature has sent you in this world with a purpose. Do not disappoint the creator by negating the potentialities of your mind body system. You must recognize the spiritual strength within you. Meditation will give you powers that you have not even imagined so far. The inner world is vast and mysterious. Explore it and you will be amply rewarded. 'When he finished, it had a great impact on the boy and he decided to visit the place frequently. Eventually he decided to join the other seekers of spirituality at the place. He asked his father the permission to pursue this goal of self-realization. Initially the father refused to give the permission but on second thoughts, considering the psychological advice, he relented thinking that at least this would make the boy happy.

This change of environment brought a positive change in the boy's outlook towards life and he became one of the brightest disciples of the head of the place. After five years the father came to know that the boy had totally changed and he was entrusted with the management of the place. Occasionally the boy was also addressing the audience on spiritual matters and he became a respected person in the eyes of the associates and followers of the spiritual place.

I have told the story to make the point that it is almost a sin to waste life in purposeless pursuits and not make use of the tremendous power lying within our mind body complex. It is our bounden duty to contribute towards the nature's purpose of evolution to higher goals of intelligent life.

***

Right Living in Competitive World

In competitive environment existing today, how far is it possible to stick to right living when competition makes people resort to means of survival that cannot be called strictly ethical or moral. We often find people making all possible efforts to make both ends meet. For them, the line between right and wrong is generally blurred. Actually, we could say that in intensely competitive situations, right living becomes more difficult. But still abandoning right living is not a correct option. I do not say that one can take liberties with rightful means for living but that it requires greater effort on the part of the individual to stick to ethical and moral ways of earning and growth. Right living in competitive world is therefore not easy and it requires skill, intellect and a determination of high order to survive and grow at the same time, keeping ethics and morality intact in their personal and social behavior. This particularly applies in working situations when rising above others your principles of life require to be sacrificed. In such situations, one could spend more energy in self-improvement than in rising above the shoulders of others.

This approach may not sound very reasonable to highly ambitious persons who justify the means by the results they achieve. For them there is nothing wrong or right in achieving their aim of high wealth and power and they have nothing to do with the ethical or spiritual aspects that may come in the way of achieving their objective. Right living obviously has no meaning for them. Right living is for those who have a conscience, a concern for others and a commitment to nature and to the Supreme Power.

Living with Strong Belief in Supreme Being

Un-shattered belief in the Supreme Being is a sign of firm faith in one's religion and an important quality of a right living person. There are many people who are religious in the sense of the word but their faith in the Supreme Being wavers as they face difficulties in life. They expect that with their faith in the Supreme Power all their problems and difficulties should vanish since they claim their religious activity will take care of God's grace on them. They however forget that there is something called Karma as well that works out the result of their past actions. The truly religious person is indeed one who believes in God but at the same time keeps this belief firm in adverse circumstances as well.

20
LIVING WITH HONESTY

Honesty is an important factor for making of a right living person. To deal with an honest person is like feeling a fresh breeze in the polluted environment of unethical ways of present life. Honesty requires purity of heart. It cannot flourish in the soil of deceit, selfish motives and maneuvering mind. Honesty is not all about financial dealings alone. We must be honest in our thoughts, speech and actions in all our fields of activity. Honesty of purpose, honesty in promises and honesty in behavior is equally important. One may bear dishonesty of a few rupees, but dishonest promises break one's heart. There are certain areas of our active life where honesty is crucial. One dishonest action can break long friendship, reliability of a person for life and so on.

As in most negative tendencies, dishonesty arises from selfish reasons. Self-gain is the motive and total neglect of the welfare of another person is the predominant factor. One may well ask why one should be honest at personal cost in a dishonest environment and the answer is in the question 'why should there be flowers in a garden full of weeds?' goodness at times may be in minority but ir outshines in a jungle of evil. Unless you are honest in pursuing your purpose, you will not be sure of success. Many times, people clothe dishonesty in sweet words but when the bitter result appears, one loses credibility forever. Some people under rate the intellect of others and resort to deceit. But most people are not so naive. They can detect dishonesty but remain silent because of their gentle nature. The egoistic persons of deceitful character may think that they can fool all people all the time but this is a mistaken belief. Sooner or later, their intention becomes clear and they suffer loss of face forever.

Unless you are honest in your actions, your ethical and spiritual component of personality has no meaning. When it is so, you are not qualified to be a right living person. When you are deceiving a person, you are deceiving God since God resides in every human form when you are deceiving God you are defying the Supreme Power. That means you have no belief in the presence of the Supreme Being this

Honesty and truthfulness generally go together though the two words have different meaning. A truthful person is more likely to be honest in dealings and vice versa. The two qualities of honesty and truthfulness are the defining parameters of goodness in a person's life. They are the basic foundation of ethics and spirituality. They arise from the presence of divinity in a person and are an indication of how good the growth of one's personality has been.

Though there may be an element of heredity in a person's development as a right living one, the good qualities are also the outcome of good training and practice of ethics and spirituality from childhood onwards. Children pick up the habit of pinching things from others out of innocent curiosity. But it is the parental advice and teacher's training that can prevent it to become a bad habit. If the son or a daughter of a shopkeeper sees his/her father short selling products to people, he/she is most likely to follow the practice in his/her own life by short changing others. It is the duty of the elders to raise the voice of conscience in their juniors.

It is not necessary that one always thinks of monetary gains for self. Life without principles may become monetarily gainful but it is not healthy for mental peace. One may not appreciate this fact easily in the rush of youth but it is the experience of aged persons which testifies to the truth of the benefits of right habits.

In the evening of life when one takes stock of one's achievements and failures, the shining moments appear to be those when one was good to one's family and good to others. In achieving these moments, it is the good qualities that were formed early in life that come to the forefront. It is said that one comes crying in the world but it is imperative that one should go smiling in the end. For that, development of good qualities is important. Honesty, truthfulness and care for others are the true qualities that can bring satisfaction to one's life. They are the three pivots for the edifice of right living.

***

Wisdom of the Enlightened

Meditation enables us to experience love and bliss by coming into contact with inner light and sound.

Pure consciousness is same everywhere and all around. Variations are the outcome of superimposition of mind and its tendencies on Pure-consciousness, resulting in its contamination and conditioning.

Our subtle being consists of our mind, intellect and the soul. Soul is the subtlest of all and it is our true self. Mind is the flow of thoughts.

In order to experience bliss, one needs to learn and perfect the art of moving beyond the premises of body, mind and intellect.

Both happiness and suffering originate in mind only.

Directly or indirectly, our every thought, emotion and feeling influences our body. Human body is subservient to mind and cannot be influenced without its consent.

God comes and lives among us in every age. But in our ignorance, we fail to recognize Him.

If you want to ask anything from God, ask the welfare of all

The greatest obstructions to self-realization are attachment and ego.

Whatever we experience and learn through the mind and the senses is not the truth.

Constant repetition of God's name brings out His grace.

A meditative state of mind must be acquired gradually or else there is a risk of becoming insane. For those who remember God and serve living beings, meditation and other kinds of ritual worship are not necessary for them.

Spiritual master is one whose consciousness is one with Pure Consciousness.

Spiritual practice brings inner awakening while senses bind us to the external world.

Human mind has great potentialities. If used positively, it can lift one to the divine level; if used negatively it can drop one into the pit of diseases and suffering.

21
NEED FOR A GURU

Success in spirituality is not possible without the grace of a guru. But one must choose the right guru. By right guru I mean one who is enlightened and has the power to show God to you. His benevolence, kindness and grace would show you the way, lead you to the right path and ultimately make you achieve your goal. Practically, all spiritual masters like Kabir, Guru Nanak and many others have emphasized the importance of guru in the spiritual pursuit. On your own, though studies and ethical and moral virtues you develop in you may help you but the seed for inner awakening is sown only by the guru. Without guru, you cannot achieve the spiritual growth to the level at which it needs to be done. He is your guide and master all the way in your journey to the spiritual goal.

Guru has to be adopted with proper understanding and faith. The first sign of the right guru is that by merely his sight or touch you will feel a sense of peace and tranquility. With his love for all, he will shower his grace on you as an act of kindness. Further, he will show you the inner light that is normally covered by your Karma and ordinarily is not seen by you. The guru has the capacity to show you its brilliance instantly.

If you cannot find the right guru, do not despair. Keep moving in the spiritual path on your own till the Divine presents the right guru before you. To some extent, you have to become eligible for the right guru by improving your Karma and this may take some time. It is an act of grace on the part of the Almighty to present the right guru at the appropriate time, so be patient and wait for the right time when you become eligible for that. You get the right guru automatically at the right time if you pursue your spiritual effort continuously. You have to purify your heart by your good thoughts, good words and good deeds. God's grace will shine on you and you will meet the right kind of guru. He will not demand any anything from you but will give you his love and advice whenever you need him.

It is said you cannot reach the goal of spirituality without Eternal Knowledge or what is called in Sanskrit Brahm Gyan. And it is the guru who provides this knowledge by his grace. What we read from books is only the information about the experiences of the enlightened ones. But without your personal experience it has no real value to make you grow on the spiritual path. You have to tread the path yourself under the guidance of your guru. Guru provides you the benefit of his practical experience and shows you the unseen sights that are impossible to see otherwise. He removes from your eyes the blinkers of worldly actions and shows you the mysteries of the inner world that we rarely try to visit. The inner world is as mysterious and vast as the outer world that enamors us. To us the inner world looks dark but the guru shows the brilliant light that illuminates it. Outwardly the guru may look ordinary but inwardly he is aligned with God and hence guru is often called God himself.

Advanced spiritual practices must also be done under the direct guidance of the guru otherwise they can harm the practitioner.

Humility is the first requirement to serve under a guru. Any amount of self-pride, ignorance or arrogance and denial of faith can never lead you to the proper growth of spirituality in you. To seek guru's grace, one has to completely surrender to him and abide by his instructions to the letter and spirit. The difference in the spiritual level of the master and the disciple often makes the disciple often ignore, doubt or question the master's command. But this is to be totally avoided because the master knows the truth and his words arise from true knowledge. One must never hide anything from the guru. The guru anyway knows all your thoughts and feelings and it is no use hiding from him your secrets. Also, one should never act smart before the guru.

All saints had had the grace of their gurus and they have acknowledged their debt to them. The practical spiritual knowledge can only be had from the guru; no matter how learned you may be by reading the spiritual literature and having the theoretical knowledge about the spiritual techniques.

***

What is Spirituality and How Does its Practice Benefits Us

This question is quite natural to arise in one's mind if one advises somebody to make spirituality a component of one's lifestyle. The answer though is quite straightforward.

Spirituality is a science of the inner world as against the science of the external material world with which most of us are quite familiar because of the technology it has generated for our comfort and ease of living. As far as the advantages of spirituality are concerned, there are many. It purifies our mind by turning us away from the negative tendencies to positive thinking. Being the science of soul, the subtlest part of our being, it opens up the whole divine world and brings its untold powers within our grasp. It sharpens our mind and intellect and enables us to face the world of actions with competence and success. It brings about a marked change in our behavior towards others since it confirms our faith in the scriptural saying that the entire world is a big family. It makes us love all the beings equally with kindness and concern. It gives us self-control over our thoughts, emotions and actions. Our outlook towards all species of creation becomes loving and benevolent. It enables us to make a direct contact with the ultimate reality of our existence. It builds confidence and energy in us to do useful work. It enhances our awareness and removes fear of death. It truly makes us a universal being that is free, confident, fearless and firm in the faith of Supreme Being. As a secondary benefit it improves our health of mind and body, especially the diseases that arise due to negative tendencies of the mind.

22
PURIFYING THE MIND

What is Mind?

In spiritual terms, it is a part of the subtle body as against the gross physical body. The other parts of the subtle body are intellect, ego, and consciousness. Mind is the reservoir of thoughts, good and bad. Thoughts lead to action and therefore, it is an important part of our psychophysical structure. Mind can take a person to spiritual heights of infinite power or take him down to the abyss of negativity and destruction. This gift of God is a double-edged weapon depending on whether we use it positively or negatively. Both conscious mind and subconscious mind originate thoughts that lead to our actions, and consequent reactions, that decide the making of our personality. The conscious mind works with sense inputs while the unfulfilled desires and emotions settle down in the subconscious and generate thoughts in our waking and sleep state. Our past actions, of this life and that of past lives, also contribute to the type of mind we possess. In this sense, our accumulated Karma is contributor to our thought process.

The conditioning of mind starts from an early age when we start interacting with the outside world. Our likes and dislike, desires, feelings and emotions as a human being, all of these contribute to our conditioning of mind. In childhood, when we are told to do this and not that, what is good and what is bad, the lessons we learn as part of education, our reactions to advices, our denials to suggestions, acceptance and rejection to the sense inputs they all form a part of our conditioning process. When we go to school and learn what is right and what is wrong, the friends and enemies we create, the behavioral pattern we adopt towards colleagues, friends and adversaries, they are all contributor to the making of our personality. The growth of negative and positive tendencies we develop as part of our experiences as well as the embedded tendencies in the subconscious due to our present and past Karma are all responsible towards our mental conditioning.

Conditioning arises due to repeated responses to worldly actions. The repeated responses become habits which are difficult to erase from mind. The mind then gets adapted to such behavioral responses and adopts them as part of our personality. Therefore, the environment in which we grow, and the stimuli we get from our senses and the reactions we give to them, all add up to make us the man we are.

We are generally inclined to have happiness, comfort and pleasure, and want them to continue; knowing full well that in nature it is not possible to have so. We live in a world of duality where pain and pleasure, good and bad, goodness and evil are integral parts of existence. It is just not possible to have what we want always. Change is the rule of nature whether we like it or not. Also, our mind always flickers. It keeps changing thoughts from moment to moment. It also it flows towards ease and comfort more easily than towards hard work and doing efforts for self-improvement. All these factors effectively create negative aspects in our life that are difficult to erase from our behavioral pattern. These are a hindrance to our growth as a spiritual being and as a right living person.

The conditioned mind is unable to take right decisions since our judgment is clouded with preferences and prejudices, likes and dislike and many other biases that are part of our conditioning. Our conscious mind is highly conditioned. In spiritual parlance, this is a great obstacle to our self-realization. On the other hand, the mind of an enlightened person is in tune with Pure Consciousness which is the unconditioned state of mind. Therefore, to achieve spiritual growth and attain the goal of enlightenment, conditioning of mind has to be removed by doing spiritual practices such as meditation or repeated recitation or remembering the name of the divine being. The latter technique is called the Japa Yoga and is an effective way of spiritualization as described in scriptures like the Bhagwadgita. The name or mantra given by the enlightened guru, or the name of the incarnation of God or simply concentrating on any name of God Himself can be used for the purpose. A rosary can be used as help.

Some enlightened spiritual gurus have emphasized the importance of de-conditioning of the mind as a path for obtaining the spiritual goal. Even if we fall short of reaching the supreme goal, the slow de-conditioning helps to purify the heart and thereby remove the negative tendencies of mind and be a person of right living. The arising of negative thoughts is involuntary and if we allow them to remain in our mind for long, they become habits and then they take us to the path of destruction and decay in personal and social behavior. The best way to get away from negative thoughts is not to allow them to linger in our mind for more than two to three minutes. We must divert our attention from them as soon as they arise in our mind. Repeated practice of this effort will ultimately kill our response to them towards actions and thereby improve our personal and social habits. Emotions like anger, hatred, jealousy and manipulative thoughts for self-gain are best avoided and ignored if we intend to lead the right kind of life. Such emotions are a result of our bloated ego and Karmic influences and are better shunned than entertained.

A completely de-conditioned state of mind is the state of Samadhi, the state of deep meditation at which union with the divine is reached. It is the state of thoughtlessness or the state of Pore Consciousness. This is a divine state and has tremendous mental powers as testified by the actions of yogis of yester years as well as the living ones. To reach that state is the ultimate objective of spiritual training. But it is not easy and cannot be achieved without the guidance and grace of a guru or the spiritual master.

Mind is like an untrained horse that has the tendency to run around here and there without any control. It can easily jump to negative thoughts, especially if those thoughts are pleasing in nature. If allowed to grow, these thoughts become natural tendencies that prove to be harmful not only to the health of the mind but also cause physical diseases since mind has great psychosomatic influence on the body.

It is said by medical experts that a lot of physical diseases are caused by mental disorders. It is now a scientifically proven fact. Further, negative thoughts lead to such actions that bring disgrace and bad name in society. Therefore, harnessing and bridling of the mind is necessary, not only for the growth of spirituality but also for leading a good normal life, a life that is good for self and good for society.

In conclusion, purity of mind is absolutely essential for right living. Mind has a tendency to roam about in good and bad pastures and therefore, it is imperative to exercise control over it for our own good as well as for the good of others. Spiritual growth is not possible without such a control. Only with a harnessed mind we can purify our psychophysical structure that will take us to success in life in true sense. With a pure mind our journey into inner and outer world will be smooth and we shall be able to fulfill the purpose of life.

***

Concern for Others

It is considered a sacred duty of everyone to help others who are needy, underprivileged, weak and helpless. This duty is a part of good social behavior in society and we are all social beings. Though everyone agrees to this and supports the idea, in practice it is rarely followed since everyone is mainly concerned with problems of own survival and growth. Some give the excuse of shortage of time while others mention the lack of resources. From right living point of view however, concern for others is an important parameter that defines the qualities of a right living person. It is as important as observing positive outlook, ethical and moral behavior and daily spiritual practices.

If we are devoted to God and also believe that God is present in all human beings, then it becomes obligatory on us to serve God by helping others. Almost everyone is familiar with the saying that service to people is service to God. Monetary help to the needy is considered charity and physical help to others is equal to worship and devotion to God. It is the spirit to help others that is important, since in practice you may be placed in a position where you have neither the resources nor the circumstances to come to help. There is also the famous line of an English poet that says 'they also serve who stand and wait. '

Sometimes we notice that some people avoid help to others because their status in society is much higher than that of those who need help. Such people want to keep distance from them because the needy come from a different stratum of society. Such an egoistic outlook is detrimental to one's growth as a right living person.

Helping others on the basis of caste or social background is not justified on the principle of equality of all human beings. Giving charity to people of one's own caste or religion only shows a narrow outlook towards God's creation. It is against ethical and spiritual principles.

In recent times a new phenomenon has come into being. People avoid helping others who are victims of accidents and trauma, fearing involvement with the law enforcing agencies that may bring time consuming court attendances and other related bothersome complications. This is causing a great hurt to society and a total lack of concern for the life of others. It is here that one's true spirit of concern really matters. Helping others even at the cost of personal discomfort and inconvenience is the true spirit of dedication for helping others. Such persons are indeed rare, though we may find many who would do charity or physical help to others in order to win some points in popularity or fame for their self-praise.

The spirit of concern for others is truly spiritual in nature if it is done in a selfless manner. Any idea of self-gain in this effort makes it unfit for the purpose of service to God. Serving people with a selfless effort is the right work that counts as service to God. It is ethical, spiritual and indeed praiseworthy in the eyes of all.

Good and Great

People achieve great heights in their professional life. Some become well known doctors, some great politicians, some others great engineers, or bankers or chief executives of industrial houses. But do all of them, or some, become great human beings? Do they develop good human values as part of their life? If they did so, the world would be a worth living place that would please one and all. On the contrary, if a bad person becomes a great politician or the ruler of the country, he/she will adversely affect the lives of so many people. History has shown this as we read about the good rulers and bad rulers. There were great kings but only a few good humans that improved the lives of people. It is therefore, not enough to be brave and intelligent and achieve the position from which you affect the lives of people. It is equally important to be kind and nice to people and work for the good of people. This is often forgotten in the race to achieve success. That is why I say it is necessary to be a right living person first and then achieve greatness.

23
Some more Bytes for Right Living

Unity—A great Asset in Adversity

The boss of a software company was in a bad mood. His wife had gone for a winter sale shopping without giving him the breakfast. He was therefore, looking for a chance to vent his anger on someone. As soon as he reached the office, he found an opportunity. A meek and humble employee had come half an hour late to the office, a fact that he found from the attendance register. He called the erring employee, and without waiting for his explanation, he shouted at him saying,' what do you think this place is? Is it a showroom where you can come and go at will? I pay you for your presence here full time and not for avoiding work. Unless you work extra time to day you will lose your salary for a day. Now don't just stand here and make me angrier. Just go and work.

The employee sheepishly tried to explain but was prevented from doing so. The secretary to the boss, who was a kind lady, hinted him to go and not aggravate the situation. The employee therefore coolly went and started his work. But looking at the downhearted state of the worker, his colleague asked him why he was so sad. He told him that he was late today because in the morning his mother became sick and he had to take her to the doctor. He knew the boss would rebuke him for his late-coming but he had no alternative. As expected, the boss did not listen to him and scolded him.

The next morning, the boss was late. The erring employee did not come. His mother had expired, and he was busy in the cremation activities. Some neighbors were helping but that was not enough. When his friends at the office knew about it, they wanted to take leave and help their friend. But the boss was absent so they told the secretary and went to help their friend. When the boss came in the afternoon and found the five employees absent without his permission, his anger rose to sky high and he immediately dismissed the five from service. When the news of dismissal reached the five, they took it in their stride and decided to stay together in thick and thin.

Five years passed.

One day the boss noticed that his company was losing contracts to a rival company and his business was going down on regular basis because the rival company always quoted less and took away the contracts from him. He asked his secretary to find out who was behind the rival company that threatened his business.

A month later the secretary informed the boss that the rival company was owned and managed by the five employees that he had sacked five years ago. They had taken the loan from the government and worked jointly. From small beginnings they had grown tall enough to challenge the well-established companies.

From then on, there was a great change in the behavior of the boss. He divorced his wife and re-established his personal life with a new beginning. His employees now found nothing to complain about. He had understood the difference between money and the money-earners that worked for him.

Q&A

Q. What is the greatest truth of this world?

A. all worldly things are perishable.

Q. what is the most difficult work in this world?

A. To control one's mind.

Q. what is the greatest achievement of a person?

A. To achieve an unconditioned mind.

Q. what is the most loveable thing?

A. Pious and pure heart and mind.

Q. what is the greatest religious work?

A. Selfless service to the people.

Q. what is the purest form of love?

A. when nothing is expected from the loved one.

Q. what is the basis of peace of mind?

A. Patience, tolerance and ability to discriminate between right and wrong.

Q. how can we be happy?

A. Be happy with what you have. Do not envy others' possessions. Avoid blaming and judging others. Happiness lies within. Do not search it outside. Contact with the inner being brings real happiness.

Divine Justice

Some people believe in divine justice and are therefore tolerant of the wrong doings of others, leaving the matter to the law of Karma which gives justice according to our actions in the world. But some, on the other hand, have no faith in the higher power and decide to award punishment to the wrong doers as a part of their social duty. The social institutions like courts and police work on the latter thinking. Belief in the divine justice generally works on the personal level and has much to do with spiritual training. In general, most people, due to self-pride, try to take revenge thinking that it is their social duty to punish the wrong doers.

Faith in divine justice is a little difficult to cultivate since belief in the goodness of the Supreme Power is a matter that requires changing of thought process. With the advance in technology people are becoming more intellect oriented and consider emotional issues like belief in God a doubtful subject. Besides, they have no time to indulge in spiritual matters since most of their time is taken by mundane matters. Also, they have no patience to wait for divine justice which has its own time frame to give results. Lack of belief in the life after death and rebirth also is an obstacle in accepting the fact of divine justice since Karma theory is inclusive of repeated births and carryover of one's Karma to future births as well.

Know Thyself

Most spiritual gurus of modern age, whether in India or abroad, get their inspiration and knowledge from the experiences of ancient spiritual masters which are either recorded in scriptures like the Upanishads or handed down verbally from generation to generation in the teacher disciple tradition going over centuries. In one way or another, they emphasize the same truth that was revealed in ancient religions. They elaborate the truth in lucid language suited to the modern thinking. Whether in Upanishads or in the Greek wisdom, the truth is stated in the words 'know thyself'. More than anything in this world, it is the wisest statement for the spiritual growth of an individual or the good of the society at large since it aims at making an individual know the eternal truth of Reality in the whole of existence. It makes every person alive pure in heart and good for the society.

Unless the individual in society is good, the collective humanity cannot be good. But unfortunately, the goodness of an individual has been ignored in preference to the interest of the collective whole. We see the deterioration in the human values in society resulting in the unhappiness of the individual but the society has never cared to improve the individual. The old sages knew that every individual that constitutes the society must be improved for the benefit of the whole. That is why they exhorted every individual in society to know oneself and realize the truth of existence. This was way to perfection of the individual and thereby the society as a whole.

Contrary to the ancient wisdom, we now advance our knowledge in science, literature, technology and so on but never care to know ourselves. Unless we act to know our true identity, we shall continue to live in disorder, chaos and confused state of mind. This creates unhappiness, loss of mental peace and general decline of ethics and morality in society. We may travel in space and advance enough to get every material possession but unless we travel within and know the inner reality our growth as a human society will be in vain. This fact has been stressed by all saints, philosophers and spiritual masters but the glamour of technological achievements and material advancement has dimmed the wisdom of the ancients in the eyes of the modern man. We can only hope for the situation to improve in time since nature is known to change with time.

A Great Advice

Below the photo of Swami Shivananda, I read the words 'Be good, Do good.' This advice summarizes the human values that almost every religion has preached to humanity. It raises our evolution from the state of animal instinct to that of a civilized person. It has been the very core and content of spirituality. To be good is the primary requirement for walking on the spiritual path. It includes all the qualities of truthfulness, compassion, tolerance, selflessness, forgiveness and concern for decency in life. Doing good includes all the actions for the good of others. In fact, doing good is the external factor of our nature and being good is the internal nature of our being. We have to be both internally and externally good to be called a right living person. This is essential to start our growth towards divinity.

Watch the Divine Presence

Watch the divine presence within you and all around you. You will marvel at the perfect mechanism with which this world is working; the nature, the beings living and non-living. A still mind that is watchful of thoughts can give you the experience. You don't need to make much effort for it except that you have to remove all undesirable thoughts from your mind and listen attentively the silent Presence in all its purity, peace and joy.

The Balance Between External and Internal

It is important to be educated and achieve professional excellence. But it is equally important to keep a balance between worldly life and the spiritual life. Never compromise on ethics and morality because it is part of your conscience and your real self. Your senses keep looking outward in the material world but once a while turn them in and explore the inner being and you will find it more enlightening, peaceful, pure and blissful.

Are we Doing Right?

Many times, we act driven by self-interest and survival instinct. We never think it as odd since we see people all around doing the same. We think this is all within the frame work of social norms that are accepted in society. Our sense of good and bad is molded by the social laws that are obeyed by the majority by the people. We never for a minute apply our mind to the consequences of our actions and leave them to the circumstances prevailing at the time. It is all due to the fact that we never listen to our conscience nor stop to think of the ethics and morality of our actions.

No doubt, it is our right to think and act for our self-existence and self-improvement. But our belief system of the past has imposed certain restrictions on our social behavior in the interest of a stable society. As per the sages' view of society, we are bound as human beings to think of all others as equal to us and take actions such that we do no harm to others. But practically what happens today? A business man does not blink an eye while doubling the price of his product to make more profit without considering the difficulty his action is going to create for the pocket of the customers. A lawyer never thinks of the society's safety when he defends a criminal. A politician hardly thinks of the effect of his selfish actions on millions of people who put their faith in his honesty.

It is all because we always want to be great and never for a moment think to be good. And what is responsible to this distorted view of life? Obviously, it is our ego that keeps us pushing to be great rather than good. We must ask our conscience what is good for us that does not harm others.

Words that Change our Outlook Towards Life

Nature tells us that in this world there is nothing that lives forever. Sages tell us that everything is an illusion and it is wrong to run around chasing the attractions of the material world. That means things are not what they seem to us through our senses. Science tells us that the ultimate reality of material objects are the quantum particles which are packets of energy or waves. Buddhist philosophy tells us that the root cause of suffering is our desires. If the objects are illusory then our desires are merely chasing illusions or we are simply chasing mirages. These thoughts of the wise people force us to take a different look on the reality of life. But to verify the truth of this reality at personal level we need to pursue long and difficult spiritual practices which are not easy for every man to do. That is why most of us live in this world chasing objects of desires and in consequence go through sufferance.

Nature Provides many Reasons for us to Be Happy

It is said in medical circles that a few minutes of anger releases in our body many toxic elements that are harmful to our health. With the same logic, one must expect that when one is in a calm or joyous mood, the body must respond in a positive way and flush out the toxicity from the body. That is why most wise people suggest that we must remain in a happy state for as long as possible. Nature helps us to do so in many ways.

From the start of the day, enjoy the beautiful sight of the sun rise. If you are near a river, hear the gurgling sound of the flowing water and the chirping sound of the birds in the morning. When you are on the shore of a sea, see the waves breaking on the shore and touching your feet. Go to a garden and see the smiling flowers and the energy giving fruits hanging from the trees. In the raining season, go out and enjoy the drizzle. It is so soothing.

If you can afford to have a kitchen garden, plant the vegetables and enjoy the fun of watching them grow. They are so mood elevating that you love them as you love your children. See the kids playing in parks and gardens and arguing among themselves on trivial matters. It is so much fun watching their innocence.

Indeed, there are countless ways in which nature makes us happy provided we care to notice with a clear mind and a clear heart.

Some Truths oLife

Even as an ordinary person we can make our life successful provided we approach life in a positive way.

Life is about doing work. To meditate and worship the Supreme are also work. Without work, Life is like death.

In Kabir's simple language, attachment and detachment in life means neither friendship nor enmity with anyone. It is unattached love for everyone. According to sages, observer's way is the best way to live.

The greatest suffering in our life is the un-fulfillment of desires. Remember, peace of mind is priceless. Do not lose it in the desire to be great.

Peace of mind is not in acquisition but in losing your negative tendencies.

Never worship God with a sense of doing business with Him, because what you have for giving to Him, He already has it and does not need your offer. What He has you are not in a capacity to absorb.

The Middle Way

Self-pride, self-esteem, self-respect are expressions which are essentially connected with individual ego. They are necessary in this world for attaining name and fame and even preserving individual existence since without these others will dominate over us and under rate our personality. They constitute the anchor for developing individual existence as a powerful man. Politicians, executives and big business men all have these rooted in them. This drives them to their position of power and wealth.

On the other hand, saints have no such ego manifestations. They have humility as their dominant trait. For them, ego is an obstacle in achieving their objective of spiritual attainment

Between the above two extreme personality traits, there is a middle path that is appropriate for a common man to adopt for living right. That path is to have limited ego manifestation for existence and earning livelihood in this practical world of conscious existence and at the same time stick to spiritual values such as truthfulness, love, compassion, forgiveness, honesty and concern for others.

In today's world, the middle path is the best way since we can no longer live as saints did in earlier times nor we can all exert enough ego to rise to material success without resorting to unfair means at one time or another. We can neither be gods nor fakirs. Let us therefore live as human beings with human values to justify our existence as right living beings.

In a Lighter Vein

An apple a day keeps the doctor away. So says the nutrition expert. But a rotten apple can cause infection for which you have to run to a doctor.

Intellectuals think head is higher than heart, both literally as well as metaphorically. But they need to remember it is the heart that supplies life giving blood to head.

To err is human and to forgive is divine. This applies to strong persons who can punish the erring one but they don't. For weaker persons, it is an excuse to evade the issue.

For every traveler in the journey of life, nature has provided a guide that we call as conscience. Do not fight it, otherwise it will stop advising.

THE SAINT Kabir said, 'Ek Noor te sub jug upja' (the universe rose from one light). Half a millennium later, scientists discovered this truth mathematically and called it the big bang theory.

God resides in every human being, so says the spiritualist. But we have covered it with a thick blanket of our Karma and then we say we can't see it.

A View

Some say God is formless, while others say He has many forms. But I don't get into this debate. For me He is everything.

Some say He has qualities, while others say He is without qualities. But I say it does not matter. Whoever finds Him he becomes one with Him.

Why run after illusions and falsehoods when Reality and Truth resides inside.

Why run after glamour and attractions when purity and wisdom are part of our inner being.

Why get confused over multiplicity of forces and images when all of them derive strength from one Supreme Power.

Why cry over hurt caused by others when the same light shines in all of us.

Why fight over the nature of One when we are all part of the same whole.

The Dynamic Universe

Our universe is dynamic every moment. The eternal energy that has created the universe is continuously in movement and change. There is nothing static in this creation. The planets are in movement, the stars are created, grow and dye, the galaxies are in continuous movement, the stars, big and small, keep producing radiation and build up material elements, the solar system itself keeps moving in the direction of the star Vega and keeps circling in an orbit round the center of the milky way, the universe also keeps expanding and the galaxies keep receding and merging and so on. In our own planet, we see movement and change all the time. The seeds are growing into plants that are going into the cycle of growth and decay. The oceans are producing clouds that take water from the seas and oceans, give it to the rivers that bring back to them. The earth keeps moving round the sun and gives us seasons to enable crops and variable weather. The day goes to night and night into the day. Even in an atom the particles are not in a static stage. All this movement in the universe teaches us a lesson. Keep moving into activity, growth and change since life is all about movement, growth and decay. The cycle of birth and death is part of this continuous change that is inherent in the creation of the universe. In fact, movement is life and stillness is death.

The Grace of God

The grace of God is priceless and comforting; it descends from heaven like a shower of nectar and falls on those who are ever absorbed in His name and thought.

It falls on the devotee like rain on parched land and gives energy to both body and mind. It lifts the soul to spiritual high and takes the person to divinely height.

This grace is not bought nor sold. It is earned through sincere effort in mind control that is determined, devotional and bold. A guru gives it free through kindness and knowledge of old.

It is the best gift of God that we can ever aspire; for, there is nothing that is so good for body, mind and soul.

Acknowledging God's Grace

In olden times, mothers used to give religious advice to their children that helped them in their times of difficulty. Belief in God was one of them. A mother once told her son, 'Always remember God is great and merciful.' The son said,' what has God given to you that you are grateful to Him?' the mother replied,' He has given you to me. What more do I want?'

A proud father was talking about his son to his old-time friend and said,' see how with my guidance and money my son has shaped into a great person.' His friend then said,' were you not the person who twenty years back prostrated before God and prayed to make your son healthy and a great official in life so that he makes a name for himself and his family? Now that God has answered your prayer, you are taking the credit yourself to boost your ego. You should truly be grateful to Him.'

An atheist friend of a priest asked him,' you are doing service to God every morning and evening and yet you have so many problems at home. Your son is ill and you have no money to provide a good treatment to him. Your wife keeps shouting at you for your ineptitude to handle the home affairs, and yet you say God is kind and merciful.' The priest replied,' my dear friend, God has nothing to do with my problems. They are the result of my Karma, the earlier actions that are responsible for my difficulties and state of suffering. The rule of Karma, or the rule of cause and effect, has been made by God for doing justice to the actions of people. God does not interfere in this rule even if you do pray to him every day. What you have done you must pay for it. As for God being merciful and kind, it is because of that that I have got this chance of serving Him so that I can improve my future through present Karma. 'The atheist said,' it is your way of looking at life. But I don't see it that way.' The priest then replied,' yes, it is my way.' The priest was right. There is always a positive and a negative view of life. It depends on you to choose what view you want to adopt in life. Cursing and grumbling takes one nowhere. Being content with what you have reduces half of your problems. The rest you tackle with honesty, sincerity and faith in the Supreme Power.

A Village Report, on a Lighter Note

A press correspondent went to a village to find the conditions there and report the financial and social conditions of the villagers of that area. As he reached there, he met a farmer and the following conversation ensued:

Q. Do you live here?

A. Do you have any doubt?

Q. how much land do you possess?

A. as much as I need to make a living

Q. how much do you make in a year?

A. The amount that is sufficient to make my family healthy and comfortable.

Q. Are you happy here?

A. happiness is a state of mind and it varies with time.

Q. how many crops do you take in a year?

A. As many as the available water and prevailing circumstances allow.

Q. do you have a social structure here?

A. what is that? But we do live peacefully provided no interference comes from outside.

The correspondent felt exasperated and said,' do you ever give a direct reply to a simple question?' the farmer said,' yes I used to but from last year I have decided to join politics and I find this mode of replying ideally suited to political way of answering since I have seen most leaders replying to our questions like this. The correspondent then said,' you have a bright This future in politics. I wish you well.' And he left the village without talking to anyone else.

This anecdote is added here to emphasize the point that it is not wise to change one's simple nature and clear hearted behavior in preference to make a point over others. One must stick to one's real nature and simplicity to keep up the spiritual quotient intact. The temptation to maneuver and twist words in order to look smart in the eyes of others must be controlled and curbed in the interest of right living. The tendency to score point over others is an expression of ego which must be avoided in the interest of keeping balance in one's behavior.

A Father's Advice to His Son

A small boy, holding the hand of his father, went to see the burning of the effigy of Ravan on the festival of Dussehra. When the effigy started burning, he asked his father,' papa, why do we burn Ravan every year, why don't we burn him once for all?

His father replied,' son, Ravan has to be burnt from time to time because he resides in our mind even after we burn him every year. His spirit corrupts our mind and we have to remove it every year again and again. Otherwise, his spirit will grow in us and we will become Ravan one day. Our minds need to be cleaned from time to time regularly. Don't we wash our hands every day? Similarly, we have to wash our minds of evil regularly.

I don't know whether the son understood his father well or not. But father definitely did his duty well and fulfilled his purpose in bringing the boy to the event.

The Argument Between a River and Ocean

A river at the meeting point with the ocean picked up an argument with the ocean. It said,' you call yourself great but you can't even quench the thirst of one person. There is so much of water with you but not even a drop to drink. Look at me. I provide sweet drinking water to thousands of persons and do a lot of good to humanity and other living beings.

The ocean then smiled and said,' you fool, do you know who provides sweet water to you? It is I who sends clouds to the land and the mountains who shower sweet water on them and then settle down as snow on the mountain tops. Without this, you will only be a patch of parched earth. But I do not take any credit for this since I serve the nature which is my duty. Remember, we are both servants and tools of the great Provider, call it nature or God. So be humble and do your duty. Do not ever boast of your work. '

This silenced the river and it coolly merged with the ocean.

Heaven and Hell

I have known the reality of heaven and hell. You will find both of them in this world. You will not have to go far, just visit any big city.

We only make them and create an impression in our mind. Both reside in our mind and come out by our actions.

Why do you make God responsible for creating them whereas both these are your creations. Leave the controversy about heaven and hell and purify your heart. Then you can win the heart of God and you can make heaven anywhere

First win your mind then only you can get the entry in heaven. Otherwise, wherever you go you will spread the hell.

Luck and Effort

Two friends were arguing on the point 'what is more powerful, luck or work?' one was vehemently defending the role of luck and said without luck nobody can succeed. The other was equally vociferous about work and said work was necessary to achieve success. When they could not decide by themselves, they approached their common friend, an aged man, who was well read and was considered wise among them. When they put the question to him, he said,' you both are right because it is your work that makes your luck. If you have good luck that means you did good work in your past. Bad luck means you have not been careful about doing good work in the past or done some bad deeds earlier. Therefore, never blame your luck but think of doing good work always.'

This explanation silenced both the arguing friends.

Some Views

Because of suffering in the world, one seems to be sad and displeased with the world. If you love the creator of the world, your life can change.

The debt to God, parents and brothers and sisters cannot be repaid for it is beyond your capacity to do so.

Mother's love, God's grace and friends' help is always pleasing. Disrespect to mother, insult to God and jealousy towards friends always brings sorrow and suffering.

Even though there is lot of suffering and evil in the world, yet there are people who create belief in the goodness of others.

Love, knowledge and happiness always increase the more you distribute to others. Hatred, anger and cruelty create suffering and hurt to others the more you spread them in the world.

In this world everyone wants pleasure but not all agree to introspect and purify their heart and mind.

In this sweet and sour world there is only one eternal truth and that is the quality less, formless Supreme Being.

Do not Blame Anyone for your Misfortune

'I think this world was made not for the simple and straight but for the cunning and dishonest' so said a person in disgust to his friends after suffering at the hands of his street-smart colleagues. However, one of his real friends felt hurt at the mental state of his friend and said,' I do not think you are right in judging people in this way. No doubt, the street-smart people have an upper hand in this world, but the simple and straight also have their place in society. I think it all depends on the environment in which you grow up and form your opinion about others.

Hearing this, another colleague said,' God did not create complications in our life. It is our own Karma, our inborn and acquired mentality, which is responsible for the way we act and think. When man is born, he is indeed without the ills that are seen in the world today. It is his conditioning, heredity, and the play of ego that turn him into the complex personality that he gets in adulthood. The survival instinct brings selfishness, and the ego brings a sense of domination over others. The pursuit of power and wealth is a direct consequence of one's ego and ambition. With all this, we still have people in this world who do not pursue this line of thinking and shun the name and fame and live the life of renunciation. They are also the creation of God. Therefore, do not blame anybody and live the life you want to live.'

Our Attachment to Life

It is a matter of great surprise that those who are unfortunate to face suffering most of the time in suffering refuse to leave the world when the time comes. They still want to cling to their physical existence even if it is nothing but pain and suffering. It is perhaps due to the instinct of survival that nature builds in our body and mind.

Many persons however, have taken steps to break the cycle of birth and death and worked for the soul related immortality as spiritual literature tells us about the early saints and sages. Perhaps they too realized that it was no fun to continue the drudgery and suffering birth after birth.

Not everyone is fortunate to have happiness and fun all one's life. Even the most fortunate ones face difficulties in life some time or the other during their life time. As Buddha realized, suffering was a reality and part of everyone's life. That is why he tried to find a way out. He did find the answer but not everyone followed his prescription. Perhaps the solution was too difficult. How many persons can meditate long hours and clean their conscious and subconscious mind? Maybe it is one in a million. It is therefore, no surprise that majority continues to suffer and clings to the mirage of happiness with hope for the future. The saving grace however is that we get crumbs of happiness once in a while that makes us forget the pain and live again hoping for the best. We continue this play of nature from birth to birth and keep grumbling about suffering in every birth. We never realize that we are a bunch of molecules that keep changing their collective shape in every life. We call it our body and are proud of it. We never think or understand that these molecules keep changing their collective shape from time to time and there is nothing permanent about it. Once upon a time, the atoms of these molecules were in the belly of a star long ago that on explosion dispersed them in the solar system. We live in illusion and remain happy in ignorance. Hence, we keep suffering but stick to life in sheer hope.

The Supreme One

A brilliant spark of light, it is the first identity of the Supreme One

The eternal truth, it is the second identity

The inner being, it is the third identity

The power of the soul, it is the fourth identity

The spiritual power, it is the fifth identity

With all these identities if we do not recognize Him, it is our fault. He always walks with us but we only recede from Him. And we recede so much that we start negating His presence. What more can be so distressing than this? It is in our own interest to know His power and remember Him in our difficulties.

If we find fault in everything, we can never find goodness in us.

Truth is self-luminous. There is no need to uncover it.

Everybody knows the difference between I and you. But to erase this difference is man's greatest achievement.

For a Good Life

Be thankful to those who gave your life and thereby a chance to improve your Karma.

Forgive and forget those who hurt you in any manner.

Love those who gave you moments to rejoice.

Remember those who shared their life's journey with you.

Be in gratitude to those who gave knowledge to you.

Be in debt to those who helped you in crisis.

Never lose faith in the Supreme One. He never lets you down even if the help is late in coming.

Your family is the ultimate support you can rely on in times of difficulty.

Every deed that you do it comes back to you with its result, whether you like it or not.

Never blame others for your faults.

Your opinion depends on the level of your perception. Think of it when you express your likes and dislike.

Some More Q&A

What is the location of heaven and hell?

They are here only. If you have jealousy, hatred, hypocrisy, deceit and anger in your heart, you create hell all around you. On the other hand, if you have love, forgiveness, tolerance and you see God in everything around you, you live in heaven and spread it wherever you go.

How to lengthen the period of our happiness?

The life of happiness gained by giving is longer than the life of happiness by receiving from others.

How do we give meaning to life?

We give meaning to life by giving a purpose to life. A scientist's discovery gives name to him and helps to increase world's knowledge base. A business man makes money for self and gives employment to others. A yogi attains spiritual height for himself and gives spiritual strength to others by advice.

If Karma decides your fate, then how to ensure you do only good Karma?

The thumb rule is that your action should not hurt anybody. However, if you want advice, the besides listening to the saints, sages, guru, and your parents, you should listen to your conscience which in most cases guides you correctly.

Truth and Untruth

To search for truth should be your duty and aim of life. Untruth can never give anyone the satisfaction and peace of mind.

Truth has immense power. It stands the test of time. Untruth gives only momentary power and fades with time.

Truth is bitter but beneficial. Untruth looks pleasant but gives sorrow in the end.

Truth takes time to win.

God's existence is in truth. Untruth is illusory.

Truth is self-luminous. Untruth prevails in darkness and ignorance.

Truth does not need any support. Untruth needs a dirty mind.

Truth cleans mind and intellect. Untruth gives birth to cruelty and harshness.

Truth is cool and clean water. Untruth is muddy water. Both flow in this world but one cleans while the other muddies it.

For your Own Good

If you want to earn respect of others, first learn to give respect to others.

If you want to win the love of others, first learn to love everybody.

If you want to win over others, first win yourself. By that is meant winning youe own heart and mind.

If you want to advise somebody, first build your trust in him.

If you want to tell others what to do, do it first yourself and gain the experience of doing it. That will infuse confidence both in you and the other. The same applies if you advice others not to do something.

If you care for others, others will care for you by the law of mutual attraction.

If you are angry and full of hatred for others, remember that you are just a bunch of molecules like others.

24
Summing Up

It is common knowledge that a human being is essentially composed of three parts; (i)the gross physical body that has life in it and is able to do physical work that involves movement and action, (ii) the subtle mind and intellect that constitutes thought that initiates intellectual work, emotional reactions, creates desires and so on, and lastly (iii) the soul, the subtlest part, that is behind all the senses, imparts the divine tendencies and spiritual outlook. For a fuller life and right living, it is necessary to nourish all the three parts, without which the life becomes unbalanced and incomplete.

We nourish the body and obtain vitality in life through food, exercise, and at times chemical and herbal inputs that keep the body fit and fine. From time to time our body reminds us its necessities and we try to comply without any arguments, delays or denials.

We nourish our mind through study, reflection, advice and introspection. We set our goals of life with the use of intellect and fulfill them with proper effort. We learn about the right objectives, desires, and avoidance of pitfalls in life, with the help of proper thinking, foresight and various other mental efforts.

Mostly, our body, mind and intellect constitute our entire worldly life since we devote our waking and sleep hours largely in fulfilling the demands of these parts of our constitution. We rarely make any effort to nourish our soul through spiritual thought and action. This denial of spiritual effort creates a deficiency in our psychophysical structure that causes an imbalance in our living style that is neither right nor desirable. The spiritual input, in fact, is not only necessary but essential to our existence as a right living person. Our ignorance of this aspect and noncompliance of spiritual effort leads to sufferance in many forms. We start neglecting ethics and morality in our thoughts and actions, we create a belief system that is in contradiction to nature's working and we start accepting greed, wastage, negative thoughts and unhealthy practices as normal to our life. These negative tendencies in turn, lead to sufferance of body and mind and we start living an unhealthy way of life.

From times immemorial, our sages and religious philosophers have been stressing the importance of spiritual aspect of our life and the need to nourish our soul. But our worldly desires, attachment to attractions and glitter of life have often come in the way and have taken us away from the need of spiritual up lift. We blame lack of time, the pressing needs of family welfare and our physical demands of pleasure and comfort for making us abandon or ignore the spiritual effort. Such pretexts and excuses only aggravate our sufferance; with the result that we blame our destiny for sufferance whereas the fact is that it is our own actions that make our destiny. Our ignoring the nourishment of soul makes us lose our peace of mind and good mental health that result in various body ailments.

The question arises, how to feed our soul. We feed our sour soul through positive thinking, developing faith in the Divine and exercising control over negative tendencies, developing a healthy outlook towards the advice of the sages, doing spiritual practice at least every morning and evening by sparing a few minutes for the meditation and Jap yoga and lastly caring for the whole humanity instead of our near and dear ones alone. Bringing purity in thought is as essential in spirituality as eating food for the body build up. Concern for nature and universal outlook in thought and action are also important for leading the right kind of life. Widening the area of our conscious behavior to include the connection of our inner being with the divine is also both beneficial and necessary. Developing a healthy respect for the Supreme Power elevates our mind and soul and improves our personality as a complete human being.

www.ingramcontent.com/pod-product-compliance
Lightning Source LLC
LaVergne TN
LVHW091319150826
845673LV00006B/1698

* 9 7 9 8 8 9 2 3 3 9 0 9 4 *